Values from the Heartland

STORIES OF AN AMERICAN FARMGIRL

Bettie B. Youngs, Ph.D., Ed.D.

Health Communications, Inc.
Deerfield Beach, Florida

Library of Congress Cataloging-in-Publication Data

Youngs, Bettie B.
   Values from the heartland: stories of an American farmgirl/Bettie B. Youngs.
      p. cm.
   ISBN 1-55874-334-0 (hard cover). — ISBN 1-55874-335-9 (trade paper)
   1. Youngs, Bettie B. 2. Farm life—Iowa. 3. Iowa—Biography. 4. Values—United States.
I. Title.
CT275.Y65A3 1995
977.7′033′092—dc20
[B]
                                                                              95-10365
                                                                                  CIP

© 1995 Bettie B. Youngs
ISBN 1-55874-335-9 trade paper
ISBN 1-55874-334-0 hard cover

Publisher: Health Communications, Inc.
                3201 S.W. 15th Street
                Deerfield Beach, Florida 33442-8190

Cover illustration and design by Andrea Perrine Brower.

Igniting the light—
the goodness—
inside

Contents

Acknowledgments

Writing this book was a very loving experience. For the parents they are—in good times, bad times, all times—I wish to acknowledge my parents, Arlene and Everett Burres. The honorable actions and intentions of these loving people transcend their transgressions. My parents have been a stable and supportive anchor in all the years of my life, and I am grateful for that. I have traveled the world over, time and time again, and find that the time-honored values their lives reflect offer a valuable blueprint for emotional, spiritual, intellectual and physical well-being. That's a pretty powerful statement. I believe it to be true. Thank you, Mom and Dad, for all your day-after-day parenting, year after year. Thank you for giving me the experience of two loving parents under the same roof throughout childhood—I had no idea how difficult this is to pull off. Thank you for bandaging up all my physical wounds and for comforting my emotional ones—and for not being the cause of either. Thank you for the depth and breadth and richness of the friendship we share. Thank you for allowing me to be all things with you—fragile, powerful; to come for advice, to be needed for advice. Thank you for your example of authenticity, simplicity, self-discipline, courage. Thank you for knowing me so well; thank you for loving me in spite of knowing me so well.

A very special thank you to those who *urged* me to write this book. Without your support I might not have. Why would stories of origin in the heartland, used to illustrate a point at a presentation, be of interest to anyone other than those attending the conference, seminar or workshop where I was speaking? A story I had written about my father in *How to Develop Self-Esteem in Your Child*, a previous book, provided insight. This piece, often called "Why I Chose My Father to be My Dad," has been reprinted many times in both books and journals, and readers have been very vocal about what the story means to them. Thank you for your explicit and impassioned feedback, and for asking me to "write more."

When longtime friends and colleagues Jack Canfield and Mark Victor Hansen asked if they could use this same piece for their book, *Chicken Soup for the Soul*, and wrote me from nearly every international airport to see if I would write additional stories for their new book, the seeds for this book were sown. For all your nudging (and support over the past 15 years), a loving thanks to Jack and Mark—you guys have always been on my A-list. To friends who offered love and nourishing friendship throughout this project: dear friend Larry Mabee, who called from an air phone somewhere over Versailles to share his feelings on a recent chapter; and Christopher Castillo, Mary Louise Martin, Mary Willia, Tom Dixson, Paul Thoryk, Tom Groff, Suzee Vlk, Sam and Jamie Raime, Bill De Leeuw, Deb and Matt Leone, Rog Norman, Christine Ferran, Tom Sharrit, John Moore, Jenny Hawkins, Steve Lorber, Gus MacNaughton, Paul Tammen, Jim Doane, Karen Zovanji and Sandy Shapery, who were ever so supportive throughout this project, and whose loving actions speak louder than any words.

Eleanor Rawson, a valued friend and senior editor at Simon & Schuster, read each of my stories as they were written, and asked if she could share them with her children and grandchildren. Her "You MUST do this book" was greatly valued. It is with respect and honor that I thank this legend in the publishing world for her encouragement and support.

A busy speaking schedule kept me on the road more than at my computer; this, too, had its advantages. As I shared a story with conference attendees and talked about the inherent value, they listened and, in return, eagerly shared their understanding of why children eventually replicate their families' values. From these participants I learned—on a deeper level—that while as a society we must all constantly monitor family wellness and support efforts designed to offset the debilitating effects of family dysfunction, we must also focus attention on those positive elements of family life and build a case for promoting the goodness and wellness that results. Most of us learn more about goodness and seek to become compassionate when we hear stories about goodness and compassion—rather than stories of hurt and evil. So to those unsung family members and others who quietly go about creating environments where good things happen, where a soul is nourished and offered fuel to soar, I send to the heavens an unending prayer that you will continue to do those things that help children develop an inner wholeness that makes their outer lives joyous and purposeful. If enough of us do this, we can make the world a safer, kinder and more accepting place during the time we fellow travelers spend in it. World peace has its origin in the simple truths children learn at the knee of a mom or a dad, or someone acting in a caretaking capacity.

A very special thank you goes to my sisters and brothers, Judy, Mark, Kevin, Tim and Laurie. I admire each of my siblings enormously. Sometimes I think that I am energetic and courageous, until I see the different and various crosses each of my brothers and sisters has been given to bear, and watch how each has worked through a particular difficulty in an honorable way.

They are the kind of people who go about their tasks thoughtfully, with integrity and in their own private way. Perhaps no other relationships we form in life, parents included, exist for as long as do those with our siblings. In childhood my brothers and sisters were partners in love and war, justice and crime, in secret keeping and in tattletaling, as you will no doubt detect from some of the stories. They recently read my recollections; to my surprise, they had nothing to add—and better yet, asked that nothing be deleted! Playfully, I thank them and look forward to expanding our relationship throughout our lives.

And finally, a warm and heartfelt thanks to my publishers, Peter Vegso and Gary Seidler of Health Communications, for having a mission in their publishing company to develop our hearts and not just our heads; may such a noble vision help our hearts evolve in ways that allow our actions to create genuine significance and purpose in both our personal and professional lives. Thank you also, Peter and Gary, for seeing the value of sharing a manuscript with readers that is so highly personal and for your encouragement throughout this task. A special thanks to the talented staff at HCI, especially Christine Belleris and Matthew Diener, for their sensitivity in editing and preserving the integrity of this manuscript. And to you, my readers, my hope is that you enjoy this book, and that the stories trigger your own positive and affirming recollections of childhood—and that the lives of these positive energies are extended and given back in the form of acts of kindness to others.

It is with admiration that I acknowledge Dic Youngs, a lifelong confidant and father of our darling daughter, Jennifer. Dic has always believed in me and encouraged me. Like his honor, his loyalty is without repute. I am a better person because Dic and Jennifer have been an interdependent part of my life.

And finally, to the most precious relationship I've ever been called upon to understand, give to and grow from: my dear daughter, Jennifer. This passionate and soulful young woman has always had a direct line to my heart and soul; she is a vital source of inspiration. And to my growth.

Introduction

I was at first reluctant to write this book, thinking that I was still too young to see how values gained in childhood played out in my life over time. In no way did I want to set myself up as example of a model citizen; like everyone else, I'm going about my life in my own way, learning as I go. Also, I didn't know how to reconcile those things about my childhood that I didn't enjoy with those I did. For example, as a child I was absolutely convinced that my placement in the heartland was a colossal, universal mistake. I found the winters too cold, the springs too wet, the early part of summers too humid, the late fall too windy and cold. (Luckily, late spring and early summer and fall were *very* beautiful. There are few redeeming things I can say about winters except that it was a beautiful sight looking out the window when standing next to the fireplace. Oh, and the icicles were spectacular.)

There were others challenges, too. There were six kids in my family; four too many if you asked me! We were expected to work together and play together harmoniously, though each of us had distinctly different personalities. I was child number two (nicknamed Bobbie, because I was supposed to be the boy), and was expected to provide leadership to those siblings younger than me. In childhood my older sister was extremely mischievous, so my reward for being such a responsible kid was that I was given her leadership roles, too. With a great deal of certainty I can tell you that after 15 years or so of doing this, I found consulting with Fortune 500 companies not at all difficult! And then there was the responsibility of numerous chores to do, morning and evening—but this was no excuse for not having homework completed or not getting to school on time, nor did it provide an excuse for not doing well in school! When my sweetheart—three years older than I and the most eligible bachelor in town—presented me with a diamond ring and a marriage proposal upon graduation from high school, I was flabbergasted. Marriage would offer more of the same. I was really motivated to go off to college! Nothing could have slowed my going, and nothing could stop me from being successful once there. I knew what the alternative offered.

My curiosity about life took me everywhere. The world seemed so vast and yet so small. And so very exciting. I wanted to go play in it, to experience it. There was within me a need to stand on the equator, to straddle it, one leg on each side just for the "feel" of it. I wanted to soar in the air in a hang glider, parachute from a plane, snorkel in the Seychelles, touch the lava beds deposited by the volcanoes on the island of Hawaii, touch an Alaskan glacier. I needed to look into the depths of the Grand Canyon, to see for myself the height of Mt. Everest. I needed to sense, firsthand, the caste system in India and the crowds of New York. I needed to visit Stavanger, Norway, the home of my ancestors, to get a feel for what living there must have been like.

I wanted to converse with young minds and old minds, and know how their learning and forgetting differed. I wanted to know what became important to me and *how so*; could real learning be derived from thought alone, or need it be experiential? Was hearing as good as touching? Was seeing believing? I wanted to know why humans come to believe as they do, and for what reasons a deeply held conviction could be abandoned or replaced by another. I wanted to know what united people and what caused them to polarize. What did business, industry, government and education have in common. How did they differ?

I was busy learning in every way. I was joyous and excited about life and all it offered (I still feel this way). I was off to see the world. Everything was possible. Everything was fresh. And without tarnish. My heart and head were void of any limitations: my parents had passed down no biases of people or places or things.

I had earned two doctorates and traveled and worked throughout some 60 countries by the time I was 29 years old. I had married my best friend and had a daughter. By the time I was 30, I had held leadership positions in business and education, and extensive contracts with city government. While I learned a great deal in these positions, the real crown jewel was what I learned from the *people* in these organizations. Always, it seemed, great masters, people of substance, those with emotional, intellectual, spiritual and physical health in abundance, were placed in my path. The likes of Joe D. Batten, Vic Preisser, Gerald Conley, Barbara Wickham, Marie Fielder, J. Bruce Francis—people of character whose lives held few contradictions—those who believed that how people behaved with family members in the homeplace was key to how they interacted with others in the workplace (and the ethics of their homes were identical to the ethics under which they conducted their business). "It's one and the same," they said. That made sense to me: my parents had worked together, played together, shared a love that focused on each other, cooked meals together, raised children together, made decisions together, struggled and succeeded together. I knew well the "one heart" theory and the benefits of cooperation and synergy, and of doing. In my childhood a good work ethic and the pursuit of excellence were expected: achievement and satisfaction were natural outcomes. As an adult, I was attracted to people whose lives radiated the same energy. There were no shortages of them in the heartland. Wonderful people believed in me, opened doors for me, encouraged me, mentored me.

Even so, I have not always made wise decisions. I have my share of distractions (and my share of detractors). I have also come upon those characters who lived on the edge of the line dividing black and white, who operated in the gray zone. Sometimes I found this lot exciting—especially if they exuded charisma, energy and passion. Childhood had shown me the positive force of those emotions as well. Shades of gray can be dangerously exciting—but over time grow tiring. They are also dangerous to one's conscience; keeping in place the boundaries of what is right and what is not right enough—while quite possibly a yoke we humans bear as a result of the infamous day with Adam and Eve and the apple in paradise—is all important to mental wellness. As I discovered when I allowed myself to be talked into visiting the ice-cream truck (as related in the story "Member of the Gang," which is included in this book), chaos, dissonance and broken relationships result from living "gray." Ken Blanchard is right; there is no pillow as soft as a clear conscience.

As I went about a very busy and involved life, I began to see the real value of having grown up in the heartland in a community that valued and promoted a principle-centered lifestyle. For example, in the early '80s I found myself living and working in a large city. More and more friends and colleagues lamented the increasing difficulty of preserving innocence for the young; of helping them find meaning and purpose; of safeguarding them from the dragons of life, and keeping children safe and on track toward worthwhile and productive goals; of preserving commitments in marriage; of finding employees with sound ethics. If institutions showed the strains of shifting social mores, they were second place to the erosion felt in the homeplace. And, illusive as they seemed, inner joy and happiness quickly began a downhill slide on a personal level as well. I could feel it, too: in the city where I lived rarely did neighbors (more and more transient) introduce themselves to each other. Children, it seemed, had lost their status as "gifts from God," and childhood no longer existed as a special period in life when we adults took the needed time to guide children, to teach patience and gentleness, and model love and tolerance in action. In fact, if children wandered into someone else's yard, they had a greater likelihood of being ignored or scolded than being walked back to their own yard and returned to their parents.

More and more, it seemed, children misbehaving in public were left to their own devices rather than called upon to examine the appropriateness of their actions. Rarely did adults enter into the lives of children other than their own (though even that was in question). This was very different from the community in which I grew up where the African proverb, "It takes a village to raise a child," was alive and well. As an example, when I was in high school, two cherished classmates died; we young people faced the challenge of dealing with this tragedy—but not on our own. In fact, our community was not only involved in helping us heal, but in their own way monitored how this experience altered their children's belief systems. Community members seemed quite attuned to the notion that youth is typically a time to test the validity of values, to determine which ones will be embraced and which will be rejected or replaced with another. In our various religions, we children had been taught to believe in God as all-loving and all-giving; He was an all-benevolent heavenly Father. Yet God had just recalled our two healthy friends and classmates. This duplicity was a big one for us young people, who on the one hand wanted to believe in the goodness of God, but who now questioned if maybe God was selective in His benevolence. Should we reject this God, or the notion of our parents as wise and all-knowing? The community read our quandary and came to our rescue. While we children reeled in our grief and questioned God, the community rallied around us, holding us, loving us through our pain, reassuring our hearts that it was right to sustain our trust in God, and encouraging us to understand the real meaning of God in times that challenged faith. They helped us realize that God does not will fate, humans do.

Growing up in the heartland, there was an expectation of living a principle-centered life. Now after more than 20 years in my field of raising expectations and stimulating excellence and achievement in both adults and youth, I know firsthand the importance of heartland values (especially being exposed to them in the formative years). I'm convinced, for example, that spending time with one's parents allows children to *really* know their parents, and that this knowing creates not only a bond of love but of understanding, compassion and respect between parent and child. Being deprived of adequate and nourishing time with our parents is not only at the heart of the men's (namely boys with their fathers) movement, it is the major epidemic we face in America—it is a primary cause of family dysfunction and erosion, and a major contributor to an inability to commit with integrity (such as in marriages or to employers) or, on a personal level, to trust ourselves.

After teaching and working with youth and families for many years, I have learned a great deal about the nature of families. I fully believe that our society mirrors the wellness of families, just as much if not more so than the other way around. There is a difference, for example, in those children whose parents substitute things for time (time offers emotional security, the real substance of durability). I have come to understand that limited possessions are not about deprivation, but rather are vital to a child's development of curiosity and creativity, and a must in retaining a sense of awe, wonder, appreciation and newness. Exercising common sense and control in giving our children what they think they want, including sexual permissiveness, is a necessity in shielding our young from growing up too soon, too fast, jaded and burned out. Growing up with parents who strive to do the "right thing" in a community where it is valued and practiced is central to helping children understand what is right and just and good. As it turns out, having two parents in a loving and committed relationship who care about and for their children may just be one of the most important things we ever *do* for our children, or *give* them. Raising responsible children is more dependent upon our children having responsibilities at home and to other family members than hoping and harping that the schools teach it. There simply is no substitute for the nourishment we get from our parents' love, especially if we wish our children to feel anchored, grounded and secure. Children need parents to model stability. And more.

Though I have written a number of books for parents, I still don't have all the answers. I am intrigued by why we humans do as we do: by how we decide on a course for our lives and by what we are willing to do or not do in the course of the years we think we are given; by the importance of childhood experiences (with both parents and siblings) to our development and sense of purpose; by who influences our lives and why; by the extent to which we transform our lives irrespective of these influences through the course of our own efforts; and by the degree our lives are destined by our spiritual history. I believe that the answers to such inquiries originate in the homeplace, rooted somewhere in the history and nature of our own lives, our parents and the values we see them practice.

I may not be alone in these ideas. In 1992 I wrote *How to Develop Self-Esteem in Your Child: 6 Vital Ingredients*, a book for parents detailing the six essential building blocks for creating a foundation of healthy self-esteem in children. In one section of the book I examined some of the subtle yet important ways children assimilate values from parents. I used as an example key values I learned while accompanying my father on late-night barnyard rounds. This book quickly found its way into 14 languages and multiple printings. While helping our children develop a foundation of healthy self-esteem is of great interest and importance to parents, it is the story surrounding my father that struck the most resounding chord with readers. Often called, "Why I Chose My Father to Be My Dad," this particular story has been reprinted many times in books and magazines. Every month my publisher receives numerous letters and calls from individuals the world over who share with us how the story touched them. Most all say that the story made them cry. Some say they cried tears of sadness because they never knew their father in the way that I knew mine, and they pine because they wish they did. Some say the story ignited within them a desire to become a more nourishing parent to their young—or grown—children. Others say the breadth and depth of my father's integrity reminded them of their own father, and that their tears are those of joy because they, too, loved and honored their father as I did mine, and still feel the power of that love—whether or not he is still alive.

The power of love. The power of parents. The power of principle-centered lives. If we want to know of their importance we need only observe the traffic of children. Whatever their need, they turn to parents. Sometimes with a tear on each cheek; sometimes with a secret too good to keep; sometimes with a question that won't wait; sometimes just hungry, or tired or guilty; sometimes to rest; sometimes to share an accomplishment or for support to accomplish a much-desired goal; often just to be soothed. Parents are a child's symbol of safety, of hope. Home is a place we can always return to. In our hearts, we know our parents will take us in.

Though I am not dependent on my parents, they are for me an anchor. This offers untold protection. My parents offer a wellspring that I can always drink from. Knowing them, I know something about me. I can't be bandied about by the wind. No one else need define me; I am me. The strengths of my parents—the values each relied upon in the course of their lives and taught me—shall last for all the days of my life.

A healthy community provides similar protection. There is a great deal of emotional wellness offered up in a community that empathizes with its members in up times and down times, whether it be a barnraising because of a tornado; or fall rains or early snow closing in on a farmer with crops yet in the field; or gathering together at the loss of a community member; or placing a citizen's photo front and center page of the local newspaper for an event as special (and character-building) as winning a blue ribbon for growing a hybrid rose, producing the best results in 4-H livestock or performing well in a marching band competition.

When I was young, I couldn't wait to leave a community that knew of every coming and going. Now I find comfort in living in a small town where my friends and I (and my dog) are greeted on a first-name basis, and where there is community concern and involvement for the health and well-being of its people and the environment of this little plot of Mother Earth.

I grew up in a community of physically strong and emotionally masterful women and men. This, too, has been a gift. As a child, I was spellbound by the physical beauty of each of my parents, mesmerized by their expansive intellect, intrigued by their sense of fairness, honesty and integrity, and by their desire, and need, really, to love us children, and captivated by their enormous passion for each other. I still am. And yet, it never occurred to them that their expectations for themselves would be anything less. There is a psychological as well as physical hardiness to folks in the heartland. The very basis of the Midwest is about confronting life and all it offers. Each man, woman and child is expected to live life vigorously—on a daily basis. Being dependable is the norm. This contributes to a work ethic; effort usually produces productivity, achievement, a sense of accomplishment—all elements necessary to self-efficacy, and central to a healthy self-esteem. I have come to value external and internal fortitude of people, and am drawn to those who exude it. I miss it in those who don't possess it.

As I mature, I have come to see other truths about the heartland as well. Many of the values are simple ones, yet they transcend time and circumstances; as an example, the value of "less is more." I'm sitting aboard a United Airlines flight, having just returned from my parents for Thanksgiving. During the holiday meal, we brothers and sisters talked about our lives and the ways we were unfolding. They told me that my life is just about the most exciting one they can imagine living. I agree, and yet I also admire their lives. I think about the obvious duplicity: I accepted my freedom and chose my own work and lifestyle, yet I have a real interest in the vastly different lives my siblings share living in the heartland.

This makes me think about what is *really* important in the journey of life. A board that I serve on has asked for a current résumé, and one of the tasks I must accomplish on this flight is to review mine. I take note that it is 16 pages long. In a world that values a 16-page résumé, I wonder perhaps if my mother's résumé, a paragraph in length, is really more profound than mine: devout Christian, devoted wife, loving caretaker of six children, Samaritan, community advocate, strong, intelligent and compassionate woman.

I take solace in the fact that I am young and still learning, growing and evolving in my (earthly and, as important, spiritual) journey. Though I have been an educator, administrator, university professor, executive director of one company and founder and president of another, I have the sense that I am just approaching the best of what is to come from the real substance, perhaps an expanded meaning in the mission of my life. I'm not quite sure why this has taken so long. My life is so very meaningful; I have been vigorously and joyously engaged in it. I have learned a lot. I have not been sleepwalking, or I think not.

Now I am grateful that I grew up in the heartland. Of all the places I have lived, worked or traveled in the world, it is from the heartland that I most see such values in force—in words, in actions and living through the lives of people. It is in such a place that I grew up.

This is not to say the heartland communities always produce such values, or that other communities in other places do not—it's just that these principles are commonplace in the heartland. Maybe this is why the heartland is so valued, so needed, so necessary to what we want to believe about ourselves. The heartland is in many ways America's anchor. There, strength, character, courage and commitment are known, proving that we as a people are capable of them, that we will rise to the occasion, that we can be counted on. As a result, we trust that we can, and will, endure. There is "wind beneath our wings," and we can trust it to carry us to the destinations of our dreams and goals, to persevere in times of crisis, to demonstrate brotherhood and sisterhood, always revealing our finest hour.

The stories in this book focus on some of the memorable experiences I had in growing up in the heartland, and what I learned as a result. I hope these stories hold for you, as they have for me, the magic of that "teachable moment"—wherein values and principles and other worthy ideals are learned daily in the exchange between parent and child, sibling and sibling, neighbor and neighbor, cousin and cousin, person and person, community and community.

It is my hope that these stories highlight the importance of taking note of what is good and lasting and nourishing in family life. It can be the ground work for doing good things. It is my experience that humans lean toward goodness and light. In a time when despondency, negativity, desperation and hardship abound, may we draw strength from what was good and is positive, and take responsibility for re-creating it in abundance in our own homes. Maybe we would be well-served to take time out from our parent bashing, and instead, try acting on the courage and fortitude we gained from them. It is also my experience that almost all parents, with each passing year, wish they had been more effective parents, and hope to be more and better to their children in the future. May we give them that opportunity.

In a time when keeping the family unit together, healthy and on track toward worthwhile goals can seem difficult if not impossible, I especially hope that we may be inspired to create positive experiences for our children at home and in our towns, cities and villages. It is precisely in a time of sweeping change, shifting mores and global clashing dissonance that we need to remember that the best foundation for successful living and loving is learned in the homeplace. Good times, bad times, all times—when leavened with family love and support—can provide strength of character, courage, compassion and leadership.

And our children are more in need of models than critics.

1

Graduation, Inheritance and Other Lessons

"It is with great pleasure that I present to you the 1978 graduating class of Drake University. These students have successfully completed their college studies: Michael M. Adams. Congratulations, Michael. Margaret L. Allen. Congratulations, Margaret."

He was so bullheaded! How could he not be here? He knew how much going to college meant to me. He had said, "If it's to be of meaning, it'll be accomplished on your own. If it's really important to you, you'll find a way to do it." Damn him! I fumed in my seat as more graduates' names were called.

"John C. Anderson. Congratulations, John. Bettie J. . . . "

One day he would see that I had done it on my own, I thought, and he would feel remorse that he hadn't been a part of it. I envisioned him, repentant and apologetic that he didn't actively follow me—freshman, sophomore, junior, senior . . . a college graduate.

"Burres. Congrat . . . "

There. I did it! I had made it through the vast land of ambiguity and bureaucratic hurdles. College had been a test measuring my tolerance to stress! Four arduous years, and the prized sheepskin was mine. The scroll with my name inscribed on it confirmed it. I remember thinking, Thanks a lot, Dad! I've longed for you to be supportive of me; to be proud of me; to think I was somebody special, really special. What happened to all those childhood lectures on accomplishing whatever you set your heart on? Your speeches on principles, goals, work ethics and discipline? Where were the fatherly pats on my head along the way? What was so important that you couldn't tear yourself away to come visit on parents' day as all the other parents did?

And now, a no-show on graduation day. How could your day possibly be more urgent? How is it possible that you couldn't save the day to participate in your daughter's celebration of a long and arduous goal now completed?

" . . . ulations, Bettie."

Against all hope I searched for his eyes in the sea of several thousand faces in the audience. He was nowhere to be found. Naturally. My departure for college coincided with one sister's wedding, another sister's toilet training and other routines of a large and rural family. Obviously he hadn't thought of my graduation day as anything out of the ordinary.

"Climb every mountain. Ford every stream." The song our graduation class had chosen for the theme seemed appropriately trite. And painfully incongruous.

"Follow every rainbow . . . 'til you find your dream."

One hundred and two new graduates marched across the stage that day. I was sure that every one of them had two parents wedged in the crowded audience. After all the graduates had received their diplomas, my class rose and began the long march down the aisle in the auditorium, all of us ready to get out of sweaty gowns and awkward caps and rush off to family celebrations held in our honor.

I felt so alone. Saddened. Angry. I had sent Dad two—not one, but two–graduation invitations. Didn't he know how much his approval meant to me, how crucial his recognition of my achievement was? It wasn't so much that I wanted him there; I needed him. Needed him to witness the completion of something very special, an outcome of all those dreams, ambitions and goals *he* had instilled in me.

"Dad, you are coming, aren't you? I mean, how many times does someone graduate from college?" I had pleaded.

"Our coming will depend on whether or not we're in the fields," he had said. "If it's a good planting day, we can't afford to miss it with the rains coming. We've missed so many days this spring, every planting day is critical now to the harvest. If it rains, we'll try to make it down. But don't get your heart set on it. You know it's a two-hour drive."

I did set my heart on it. It was all that mattered.

"Climb every mountain . . . " Parents, grandparents and relatives were all smiles, straining for a glimpse of their new graduate, politely shoving others out of the way to get that cherished picture, proud of their own new status as mother, father, grandparent, brother, sister, aunt, uncle *of the graduate*. Theirs were the tears of happiness; the tears I fought back were of absolute disappointment and rejection. It wasn't just that I *felt* alone; I *was* alone.

"Follow every rainbow. . . . "

I must have taken 27 steps from center stage, where I had shaken hands with the university president as I accepted my diploma—my ticket to the world in my future—when I heard the voice. "Bettie," he whispered in a soft voice that was intrusive yet urgent and private. It startled me out of my invented and suffocating dejection. The sound of my father's voice leaked through the thunderous applause of an enormous, roaring audience. I'll never forget the vision of the man before me. There, in the end seat of the long aisle saved for the spillover of graduates, sat my father. He looked smaller and more reserved than the bold and thunderous man I knew him to be. His piercing sky-blue eyes with their mass network of tiny red vessels were clouded by a liquid sheath of tears. Then giant tears engulfed and drowned those eyes, streaming down his cheeks and dropping in rivulets on a blue suit that was obviously brand new. His head was lowered slightly, his face a picture of far too many words. He looked so humble, yet so filled with fatherly pride. I'd seen him cry only one other time, but not like this. Here were big serene tears that couldn't be contained. The sight of this masculine and proud man—my father—in tears broke loose the dam of tears I had concealed behind a mask of mocked confidence.

Within an instant, he was on his feet. My emotions under siege, I reacted to that fervent and impassioned moment by thrusting my diploma into his hand. "Here, this is for you," I said, my tone a blend of arrogance, revenge, need, no-thanks-to-you, love and pride.

"This is for you," he countered in a voice devoid of anything but gentleness and love. His hand swiftly entered into his coat pocket and emerged with an envelope in it. In a clumsy gesture he reached out a huge weathered hand and thrust the paper at me. With the other hand he rerouted the tears running down his cheeks. It was a very intense and emotional ten seconds.

The procession continued. My heart racing, I tried to piece together the events of the day. I tried to imagine his thoughts as he made the decision to come, his conversation with Mom as they made the two-hour drive, his ease or frustration in finding the university, fending off graduates and hoarding a seat—far in front of those reserved for parents!

My dad had come! It was one of the most beautiful days spring had to offer, a perfect planting day. And that new suit! As I remembered it, he had bought one for Uncle Ben's funeral. One decade later, he had purchased one for my sister's wedding. A suit was considered frivolous to this farme; besides, owning one took away an excuse for not going where he didn't want to go! Buying a new suit definitely demanded a very important occasion. He was there, Dad in his new suit.

". . . until you find your dream." One of mine had come true.

I glanced at the envelope that was crushed from my grip. I had never received a note or card from Dad before and really didn't know what to think. My imagination went wild with the possibilities. Would it be a card . . . with his signature? (Mom had always signed for the both of them.) It was a rare and integrity-laden deal when E. H. Burres signed his name. Everyone knew a handshake from this man was as good as a signature. When E. H. Burres gave his word—well, it was a done deal. No banker had ever turned down my father, who, after serving two tours of duty in World War II, had started his farm life with nothing more than a dream, a good work ethic, an impeccable sense of honor, a solid sense of character and that beautiful, vibrant and loyal woman at his side. This man with all those kids and those bold dreams of owning land.

Maybe it was just an extra copy of the graduation program. Perhaps the moment had flustered him just as it had me and he simply handed me something, anything. Could it be an invitation to an assembling of the Burres clan to celebrate this day? Wanting to savor any and all possibilities, and afraid of being let down, I reserved opening the envelope until I reached the changing room. I struggled out of my cap and gown without letting go of this precious piece of paper.

"Look what my parents gave me for graduation," Martha gushed as she held up her hand, showing off a gleaming pearl ring for all to see.

"My old man gave me a car," yelled Todd, from across the room.

"Must be nice. I got nothing, as usual," came a voice from somewhere.

"Yeah, me too!" chimed in another.

"What did you get from your parents, Bettie?" yelled my college roommate from across the room.

It didn't seem appropriate to say, "It doesn't matter because my dad was there," so I turned away and pretended not to hear. I folded the graduation gown neatly and put it in the bag where it remains to this day—a symbol given life by my father's words and actions.

Tears again came to my eyes as I thought about the compassion I saw in my father's eyes. He had come after all. The completion of this goal was important to him. I was important to him. Either that or Mom won the fight! I opened the envelope slowly and carefully, not wanting to tear this precious memento from my father.

Dear Bettie,

I know you remember how, when I was a young boy, my family lost the family farm. My mother was left to raise six children, mostly alone. *It was a rough time for all of us. It was a sad day when we were notified our family farm was being taken from us. On that day I vowed that someday I would own land, and that all my children would have a legacy to this land. They would always be secure. Wherever they lived in the world, no matter what was to be their fate, there would always be a Burres homestead to come home to.* My *children would* always *have a home. The attached letter is your deed to* your *farm land. The taxes have been forever paid. It is yours.*

When I saw you go off to college, you can imagine how proud I felt, and so hopeful that you would, one day, complete your degree. You can't really know how helpless I felt when I could not stretch our family's dollar to include your college. At the time, I didn't know how to tell you that without destroying your confidence in me to care for my family. I needed you to believe in me. And it wasn't because I didn't value what you were doing, nor was it for lack of recognition of how hard you were working to make your dream come true. Though I might not have followed you as closely as you would have liked, know that you were never out of my thoughts. Always I watched you, though from afar. It might have seemed to you that I was impervious to your trials of going it alone, but I wasn't. I was coping with my own struggles of a growing family, and actualizing a dream I refused to let go of because it was so important to me—it was my legacy to you children, and involved making good on a promise I had made to God in exchange for some other things.

I prayed for you constantly. Know, dear daughter, that your strength and ability to forge ahead when all seemed against you was often the very thing that kept my own dreams alive, and renewed my strength to keep going even when my own trials and tribulations seemed insurmountable—and made them urgent and worth it. You see, it was you who were my hero, *a pillar of strength, courage and audacity. In you, I saw me. As I watched the boundless energy of your youth, and the air of arrogance that shielded you from others you thought would take you away from your dream, or convince you that it wasn't as important as you deemed it to be, as I saw that Burres pride-in-action, as I listened to your determination to complete your mission, I knew you would be all right. I knew that not only could you do it, but that you would.*

And so, today we both have a piece of paper symbolizing the completion of dreams, actualized because we have applied hard work toward noble goals. Bettie, I am so very proud of you today.

*Love
Dad*

(Author's note: His actual signature!)

2

The Little Glass Chip

Quite often my mother would ask me to set the family table with "the good china." As is often the case, china was a family heirloom, passed down from generation to generation and held in the highest regard. My mother ordered the table to be set with the china quite frequently, but I never questioned these occasions. I assumed they were just my mother's desire or momentary whims and did what I was asked.

One evening as I was setting the table, our neighbor Marge dropped by unexpectedly. She knocked at the door and Mom, busy at the stove, called to her to come in. Marge entered the large kitchen and, glancing at the beautifully set table, remarked, "Oh, I see you're expecting company. I'll come back another time. I should have called first, anyway."

"No, no, it's all right," replied my mother. "We're not expecting company."

"Well then," said Marge, with a puzzled look on her face, "why would you have the good china out? Gosh, I'd never trust my son to handle my grandmother's dishes. I'm so afraid they'll get broken, I use them only twice a year, if that."

"Because," my mom answered, laughing softly, presumably because she found it silly that Marge should use her china so infrequently, "I've prepared my family's favorite meal. If you set your best table for guests and outsiders when you prepare a special meal, why not for your own family? They're as special as anyone I can think of."

"Well, yes, but your beautiful china will get chipped," responded Marge, still not understanding the importance of the value my mother had assigned to esteeming her family in this way. "And then you won't have it to pass on to your children."

"Oh well," said Mom, casually, "a few chips in the china are a small price to pay for the joy we get using it. Besides," she added with a twinkle in her eyes, "all these chips have a story to tell, now don't they?" She looked at Marge as though a woman with a family of her own should have known this.

Marge still didn't get it.

Mom walked to the cupboard and took down a plate. Holding it up, she said, "See this chip? I was 17 when this happened. I'll never forget that day." My mother's voice softened and she seemed to be remembering another time. "One fall day my brothers needed help putting up the last of the season's hay, so they hired a strong young man to help out." Mom paused, then continued. "My mother had asked me to go to the hen house to gather fresh eggs. It was then when I first noticed this very handsome young man. I stopped and watched for a moment as he picked up the large and heavy bales of freshly cut hay and slung them up and over his shoulder, tossing them effortlessly into the hay loft. I tell you, he was one gorgeous man: lean, slim-waisted, with powerful arms and shiny, thick sandy-blonde hair. He must have felt my presence because with a bale of hay in mid-air, he stopped and turned and looked at me, and just smiled. He was so incredibly handsome," she said slowly, running a finger around the plate, stroking it gently.

"Well, I guess my brothers took a liking to him because they invited him to have dinner with us. When my older brother directed him to sit next to me at the table, I nearly fainted. You can imagine how embarrassed I felt because he had seen me standing there staring at him. Now, here I was seated next to him. His presence made me so flustered, when he asked me when I was to graduate, I got tongue-tied. I don't remember what I said!" Suddenly remembering that she was telling a story in the presence of her young daughter and a neighbor, Mom blushed and hurriedly brought the story to conclusion. "Well, anyway, he handed me his plate and asked that I dish him a helping. I was so nervous that my hands shook. When I took his plate, it slipped and cracked against the casserole dish, knocking out a chip. I handed the plate back to him, hoping he hadn't noticed."

"Well," said Marge, unmoved by my mother's story, "I'd say that sounds like a memory I'd try to forget."

"On the contrary," countered my mother. "As he was leaving the house he walked over to me, took my hand in his and laid the little piece of chipped glass in my palm. He didn't say a word, just smiled that incredible smile. One year later I married that marvelous man. And to this day, when I see this plate, I fondly recall the day I met him." She carefully put the plate back into the cupboard—behind the others, in a place all its own. Seeing me staring at her, she gave me a quick wink.

Aware that the passionate story she had just told held no sentiments for Marge, she hurriedly took down another plate, this time one that had been shattered and then carefully pieced together, with small droplets of glue dribbled out of rather crooked seams. "This plate was broken the day we brought our newborn son, Mark, home from the hospital," Mom said. "What a cold and blustery day that was! Trying to be helpful, my six-year-old daughter dropped that plate as she carried it to the sink. At first I was upset, but then I told myself, it's just a plate and I won't let a broken plate change the happiness we feel welcoming this new baby to our family. As I recall," she said, "we all had a lot of fun on the several attempts it took to glue *that* plate together!"

I was sure my mother had other stories to tell about that set of china.

Several days passed and I couldn't forget about that plate with the chip in it. That plate had been made special, if for no other reason than because Mom had stored it carefully *behind* the others. There was something about that plate that intrigued me, and thoughts of it lingered in the back of my mind.

A few days later my mother took a trip into town to get groceries. As usual, I was put in charge of caring for the other children while she was gone. As she drove out of the driveway, I did what I always did in the first ten minutes when she left for town: I ran into my parents' bedroom (as I was forbidden to do!), pulled up a chair, opened the top dresser drawer and snooped through it, as I had done many times before. There in the back of the drawer and beneath soft and wonderful smelling grown-up garments, was a small, square, wooden jewelry box. I took it out and opened it. Inside were the usual items, the red ruby ring left to my mother by Auntie Hilda, her favorite aunt; a pair of delicate pearl earrings given to my mother's mom by her husband on their wedding day; and, my mother's dainty wedding ring, which she often took off as she helped do outside chores alongside her husband.

Once again enchanted by these precious keepsakes, I did what every little girl is wont to do. I tried them all on (as I had done so many times before), filling my mind with glorious images of what I thought it must be like to be grown up, to be a beautiful woman like my mother and to own such exquisite things. I couldn't wait to be old enough to command a drawer of my very own and be able to tell others they could not go into it!

Today I didn't linger too long on these thoughts. I removed the fine piece of red felt from the lid on the little wooden box that separated the jewelry from an ordinary-looking chip of white glass—heretofore, completely meaningless to me. I removed the piece of glass from the box, held it up to the light to examine it more carefully and following an instinct, ran to the kitchen cabinet, pulled up a chair, climbed up and took down that plate. Just as I had guessed, the chip so carefully stored beneath the only three precious keepsakes my mother owned, belonged to the plate she had broken on the day she had first laid eyes on my father.

Wiser now, and with more respect, I cautiously returned the sacred chip to its place beneath the jewels and replaced the piece of fabric that protected it from being scratched by the jewelry. Now I knew for sure that the china held for Mother a number of love stories about her family, but none quite so memorable as the legacy she had assigned to that *plate*. With that chip began a love story to surpass all love stories, now in its 53rd chapter—for my parents have been married now for some 50 years!

One of my sisters asked Mother if someday the antique ruby ring could be hers, and my other sister has laid claim to

Grandmother's pearl earrings. I want my sisters to have these beautiful family heirlooms. As for me, well, I'd like the memento representing the beginning of a very extraordinary woman's very extraordinary life of loving; I'd like that little glass chip.

3

Why I Chose My Father to Be My Dad

I grew up on a beautiful sprawling farm in Iowa, raised by parents who are often described as the "salt of the earth and the backbone of the community." They were all the things we know good parents to be: loving, committed to the task of raising their children, with high expectations and a positive sense of self-regard. They expected us to do morning and evening chores, get to school on time, earn decent grades and be good people.

There are six children. *SIX* children! It was never my idea that there should be so many of us, but then no one consulted me. To make matters worse, fate dropped me off in the middle of the

*Reprinted with the permission of Rawson Associates, an imprint of Simon & Schuster, from *The 6 Vital Ingredients of Self-Esteem and How to Develop Them in Your Child* by Bettie B. Youngs, Ph.D. © 1991 Bettie B. Youngs, Ph.D. (This work was published in paperback as *How to Develop Self-Esteem in Your Child: 6 Vital Ingredients*. New York: Fawcett, 1992.)

American heartland in a most harsh and cold climate. Like all children, I thought that there had been a great universal mistake and I had been placed in the wrong family—most definitely in the wrong state! I disliked coping with the elements; the winters in Iowa are so freezing cold that you have to make rounds in the middle of the night to see that livestock aren't stranded in a place where they would freeze to death. Newborn animals have to be taken into the barn and sometimes warmed up in order to be kept alive. Winters are *that* cold in Iowa!

My dad, a strikingly handsome, strong, charismatic and energetic man, was always in motion. My brothers and sisters and I were in awe of him; we honored him and held him in the highest esteem. Now, I better understand why. There are no inconsistencies in his life. He is an honorable man, very principled. Farming, his chosen work, was and is a passion; he's the best. He was at home, raising and caring for animals. He felt at one with the earth, and took great pride in planting and harvesting the crops. He refused to hunt out of season, even though deer, pheasants, quail and other game roamed our farmlands in abundance. He refused to use soil additives or feed the animals anything other than natural grains. He taught us why he did this, and why we must embrace the same ideals. Today I can see how conscientious he was, because this was in the mid 1950s, before there was an attempt at universal commitment to earthwide environmental preservation.

Dad was also a very impatient man, but not in the middle of the nights when he was checking his animals during those late rounds. The relationship we developed from these times together was simply unforgettable; it was to make a compelling difference in my life. I learned so much *about* him. Colleagues often tell me of the sorrow and disappointment they feel about having spent so little time with their fathers; indeed, the heart of today's men's groups is about groping for a father they never *really* knew. I knew mine.

Back then, I felt like I was secretly his favorite child, although it's quite possible that each of us six children felt that way. Now that was both good news and bad. The bad news was that I was the one selected by Dad to go with him for these midnight and early morning barnyard checks, and I absolutely detested getting up and leaving a warm bed to go out into the frosty air. But my dad was at his best and most lovable during those times. He was most understanding, patient, gentle and a good listener. He was kind, his voice was gentle and his smile made me understand my mother's passion for him.

It was during these times when he was a model teacher— always focusing on the whys, the reasons for doing. He talked endlessly for the hour or hour-and-a-half that it took to make rounds. He talked about his war experiences, the whys of the war he served in (World War II) and about the region, its people, the effects of war and its aftermath. Again and again he told his story. In school, I found history all the more exciting and familiar.

He talked about what he gained from his travels and why seeing the world was important. He instilled a need and love of traveling (I had worked in or visited some 30 countries by the time I was 30 years old!). He talked about the need and love of learning and why a formal education is important, and talked about the difference between intelligence and wisdom. He so wanted me to go beyond my high school diploma. "You can do it," he'd say over and over. "You're a Burres! You are bright, you have a good mind and remember, you're a Burres!" There was no way I was going to let him down; I had more than enough confidence to tackle any course of study! Eventually, I completed a Ph.D. and later earned a second doctorate. Though the first doctorate was for Dad and the second for me, there was definitely a sense of curiosity and quest that made both easy to attain.

He talked about standards and values, about developing character and what it meant in the course of one's life. I write and teach on a similar theme. He talked about how to make and evaluate decisions, when to cut your losses and walk away, and when to stick it out, even in the face of adversity. He talked about the concept of *being and becoming*, and not just *having and getting*; I still use that phrase. "Never sell out on your heart," he said. He talked about gut instincts and how to decipher between those and emotional sells, and how to avoid being fooled by others. He said, "Always listen to your instincts, and know that all the answers you'll ever need are within you. Take quiet time alone; be still enough to find the answers within, and then act on them. Find something you love to do, and then live a life that shows it. Your goals should be aligned with your values, and then your work will radiate your heart's desire. This will divert you from all silly distractions that will only serve to waste your time. *Your very life is about time*—care how much you can be active in whatever years you are given. Care about people," he said, "and always respect Mother Earth; wherever you shall live, be sure you have full view of trees, the sky and land."

My father. When I reflect on how he loves and values his children, I'm genuinely sorry for the youth who will never know their fathers in this way, or will never feel the power of character, ethics, drive and sensitivity all in one person—as I do in mine. My dad modeled what he talked. And I always knew he was serious about me. I knew he felt me worthy, and he wanted me to see that worth.

Dad's message made sense to me because I never saw any conflict in the way he lived his life. He had thought about his life and he lived it daily. He bought and paid for several farms over time (he's as active today as he was then). He married and has loved the same woman for a lifetime. My mother and he, now married for 50-plus years, are inseparable sweethearts, still. They are the most bonded lovers I've known. Dad was a family man—and a man who needed his family. I thought he was overly possessive and protective of his children, and I certainly didn't always agree on his discipline techniques, but now that I'm a parent I can understand his actions and see them for what they were. Though he thought he could save us from the measles and almost did, he vehemently refused to lose us to destructive vices. I also see how determined he was that we be caring and responsible adults. His caretaking, guidance and discipline were instilled in six children.

To this day, five of his children live within a few miles of him, and they themselves have chosen a version of his lifestyle. They are devoted spouses and parents, and agriculture is their chosen work. They are, without a doubt, the backbone of their community. There is a twist to all this, and I suspect it's because of his taking me on those midnight rounds. I took a different direction than did the other five children. I began a career as an educator, counselor and university professor, and eventually wrote several books for parents and children to share what I had learned about the importance of developing self-esteem in the childhood years. My messages to my daughter, while altered a bit, are the values that I learned from my father, tempered with my life experiences, of course. They continue to be passed on.

I should tell you a bit about my daughter. She's a tomboy—a beautiful 5'9" athlete who letters in three sports each year, frets over the difference between an A- and a B, and was just named a finalist in the Miss Teen California competition. But it's not her outward gifts and accomplishments that remind me of my parents. People always tell me that my daughter possesses a great kindness, a deep sense of knowing and of spirituality, a special fire deep inside that radiates outward: the essence of my parents is personified in their granddaughter.

The rewards of esteeming their children and being dedicated parents have had a most nourishing effect on the lives of my parents as well. As of this writing, my father is at the Mayo Clinic in Rochester, Minnesota, for a battery of tests, scheduled to take from six to eight days. It is December. Because of the harsh winter, he took a hotel room near the clinic (as an outpatient). Because of obligations at home, my mother was only able to stay with him for the first few days. So on Christmas Eve, they were apart.

On the eve of Christmas I first called my dad in Rochester to say Merry Christmas. He sounded down and despondent. I called my mother in Iowa. She was sad and remorseful. "This is the first time your father and I have ever spent the holidays apart," she lamented. "It's just not Christmas without him."

I had 14 dinner guests arriving, all ready for a festive evening. I returned to cooking, but not being fully able to get my parents' dilemma off my mind, I called my older sister. She called my brothers. We conferenced by phone. It was settled. Determined that our parents should not be without each other on Christmas Eve, my younger brother would drive the two hours to Rochester to pick up my father and bring him home, without telling my mother. I called my father to tell him of the plans. "Oh, no," he said. "It's far too dangerous to come out in a night like this." My brother arrived in Rochester and knocked at my father's hotel door. He called me from Dad's room to tell me my father would not go. "You have to tell him, Bobbie [my nickname]. You're the only one he'll listen to."

"Go, Dad," I said gently.

He did. Tim and my dad started for Iowa. We kids kept track of their progress, the journey and the weather by talking with them on my brother's car phone. By now, all my guests had arrived and all were a part of this ordeal! Whenever the phone rang, we put it on the speaker phone so we could all hear the latest. It was just past 9:00 when the phone rang. It was Dad on the car phone. "Bobbie, how can I possibly go home without a gift for your mom? It would be the first time in nearly 50 years I didn't get her a gift for Christmas!" By now my entire dinner party was engineering this plan! We called my sister to get the names of nearby open shopping centers so they could stop for the only gift my dad would consider giving mom—the same brand of perfume he has given her every year at Christmas.

At 9:52 that evening, my brother and my dad left a little shopping mall in Minnesota for the trip home. At 11:50 they drove into the farmstead. My father, acting like a schoolboy, stepped around the corner of the house and stood out of sight.

"Mom, I visited Dad today and he said to bring you his laundry," my brother said as he handed my mom the suitcases. "Where do you want me to put it?"

"Oh," she said sadly, "I miss him so much. Why don't you just give them to me. I might as well do it now."

Said my father coming out from his hiding spot, "You won't have time to do that tonight!"

After my brother called me to relay this touching scene between our parents—these two friends and lovers—I phoned my mother. "Merry Christmas, Mom!"

"Oh you kids. . . ." she said in a crackling voice, choking back tears. She was unable to continue. My guests cheered.

Though I was 2,000 miles away from them, it was one of the most special Christmases I've shared with my parents. And, of course, to date, my parents have not been apart on Christmas Eve. That's the strength of children who love and honor their parents, and of course, the committed and marvelous marriage my parents share.

"Good parents," Jonas Salk once reminded me, "give their children roots and wings. Roots to know where home is, wings to fly away and exercise what's been taught them." If gaining the skills to lead one's life purposefully and having a safe nest and being welcomed back to it is the legacy of parents, then I believe my parents were good parents. It was this past Christmas that I most fully understood the full cycle of self-esteem in families. The roots and wings my parents gave six children will forever be an indelible foundation.

4

Red Dot

We were four spirited little children in motion, prancing around in circles, poking, pinching, playfully slapping each other, giggling and squealing, burning up the last bits of seemingly infinite energy before bedtime, or so our mother hoped. Unexpectedly, the house lights went out, followed by our mother's sudden and abrupt order: "Shh!" Just as the baby animal knows when its mother's call means "Gather around, it's time to go now," versus "Run to me, danger is lurking," we children knew precisely how to decipher the meaning behind our mother's tone of voice. Like a science, we knew when "Shh" held the possibility of a hug or kiss, or the possibility of a scolding or spanking. This was the tone of alarm, immediacy.

Eight little blue and dependent unworldly eyes darted instantly in the direction of their security, searching their mother's wise eyes for clues to explain what was happening. Inextricably bonded to this loving and protecting young woman, we implicitly trusted Mom's role as our caretaker—a responsibility she lovingly assumed. Sensing uncertainty in her voice and anxiety in her eyes, we aligned ourselves with her fright and felt it, too. Quickly, the orders were obeyed. Frightened of whatever it was that had alarmed our mother, we stood motionless in the middle of the floor, in silence, peering through the darkness to keep her silhouette in sight. Mother quietly glided to the kitchen window, staring through the blinds in the direction of the red dot coming down the lane. Curious, I whispered, "What do you see, Mommy?"

"A red dot," was her answer.

"Mama, will it kill us?" asked my three-year-old little brother, Kevin. Alarmed, he sucked on his thumb frantically.

"No, no, it won't hurt us." Mom whispered, but her voice undermined the veil of bravery she wore for the sake of her children. Unconvinced, four little bodies scampered under the kitchen table, inching and nudging closer together, as though huddling would somehow guarantee their safety. Five-year-old Mark put his finger to his lips as he had seen his mother do and cautioned his younger brother to hold down the sounds made by the little boy's vigorous sucking.

"If we're quiet it'll go away," reassured my older sister, wanting to believe—as did the rest of us—that our stillness would protect us and make our mother's fear go away.

Intended more for her own comfort than for us, Mother whispered, "Ohhh, I wish your daddy was here." I could tell that she was crying. She opened wider the tiny white blinds to get a better glimpse at the thing coming up the lane.

"Stay here," my sister Judy ordered her two brothers, grabbing me by the arm to make me come along. My sister and I crawled over to the window and crouched beside our mother, searching the darkness for the red dot that frightened her so.

This was not the first time our mother had witnessed an encroacher, nor gathered her children and stood watch over them. It had come on some nights when my father worked late in the fields harvesting the crops. I had heard my mother tell my father of this thing. And Dad had dealings with the red dot, too. On several occasions, down came the trusty old Winchester and a shot or two would be fired into the air as a warning. That was usually enough.

How I wished that Dad were here now. If he were here, our mother wouldn't be fearful. And we wouldn't be hovering in the dark. But Dad would not be coming to our rescue tonight; he had gone to buy livestock at an auction nearly 200 miles away and would not be back until the early morning hours. Tonight my mother faced the intruder with four small children and a baby on the way.

We were living on a farm near Vincent, Iowa, at the time, a very beautiful homestead with a big yard, lush trees and flowers everywhere my mother could find a place to plant a seed. Which was everywhere. Gorgeous purple and white morning glories climbed the siding on three sides of the house; thick beds of marigolds added their coordinated hues of sienna brown, rust, orange and gold blooms to sheds and outbuildings. Pink and pale purple hollyhocks sprouted along the front of the barn, along the fences going down the half-mile-long lane and beside the big mailbox with the family name painted in white capital letters: BURRES. As was sometimes the case in rural life, a thief would come onto rural folks' farms in the late dark of the night, looting a shed, or stealing a chicken or goose. Gas was perhaps the most valued commodity, though shovels, axes, machine tools and even livestock sometimes disappeared.

"You girls can stay here at the window only if you are very quiet," my mother warned. "But, boys, you must stay there under the table and be very quiet." Teddy, the dog member of the family, was on the porch—aware that something was not quite right here. His brown gentle eyes were framed by an enormous skull and covered with a beautiful chocolate, yellow and white mane of long collie hair. Sensing trouble, Teddy scanned Mom's face to better understand what she knew and to get direction for what he should do—should he lie low, or begin a crusade of barking? My mother looked at Teddy, and then to the shadows of each of her four children and back to the dog. He understood perfectly her unspoken thoughts; he would be silent for now. With vigilant ears pointed in the air, Teddy crouched down and, resting his head on outstretched paws, continued his watch of the lane. Attentive and heedful, his energized body was ready for action. This was his family, and he was guarding it.

Teddy had come to our family by way of a Christmas stocking when he was six weeks old. It was a smaller family then, just two adults and two little curly-headed, freckled-faced girls. He had been with our family nearly six years now and had watched it grow larger and noisier. His role of getting and giving love expanded every time a new child was born. It was a big job, but he was up to it.

There was never a dull moment. It was his daily chore to help Dad corral the livestock in the morning and bring the cows home each evening. He walked the older children to the bus and dutifully pined until they returned. Mom always called him to walk with her down the lane and back to get the mail. And she expected him to sit on the front porch by the door and guard the house when she went to town.

Some of our family members needed him more than others. When the smallest of the children cried because the rest of us left for school, he was needed as a comforter and sometimes as a pillow to curl up with, until the small child was adequately distracted from his loss. When my mother reached for a washcloth to wash the baby's face, he dashed over and licked the child's face to save her a trip.

Yes, sir, he knew our family well; knew *all* our quirks. He knew how to play us to get what he wanted, too. Experience had proved that if he sat proudly when Dad was milking the cow, following the gruff, "What ya doing, Teddy!" fresh milk would be squirted directly from the cow's udder into his mouth. Then Dad would laugh and talk to him some more. Around about the time the sun started to come up in the east or set in the west, wonderful aromas poured from the house, and he would check the old screen door. A wooden clothespin wedged at the bottom meant that four kids were about to become accomplices to his hideout under the kitchen table. Mom forbade animals in the house, even if they were members of the family. With a paw or nose, he would slyly open the screen, watch carefully for Mom to turn her back, and then dutifully dash under the table where he hid out illegally and was fed illegally, too.

When we children were put to bed, he'd sit beneath our window and with a low-grade whine, whimper until we opened the window, removed the screen and by hair, head or available leg, hoisted him up and into our bedroom. No matter how much pain we lovingly inflicted, he endured it, gladly. And he was smart. He knew when the footsteps coming down the hall belonged to Mom or to Dad and knew exactly what to do when the word "Go!" was issued by one of us children. "Go!" meant he was to disappear under the bed and lie there silently until the big pair of feet left the room. He knew "It's clear!" meant it was safe to come out. Content with his leadership role by day, he didn't mind being our puppet by night.

"What *is* the red dot, Mama?" Mark wanted to know.

"Mom, please tell us," begged nine-and-a-half-year-old Judy.

"It's a man smoking a cigarette, walking up our lane," she whispered.

"Why?" the baby asked. His question went unanswered.

"Let Teddy go get him," Mark said with an air of confidence. "He'll chase him away!" Hearing our voices, Teddy slid closer to the window, as if to reassure us that he was ready to go upon command.

"No, he may hurt Teddy," replied Mom.

"Nobody would kill Teddy," my sister countered matter-of-factly, as though saying so was built-in protection. My two brothers and I shook our heads in agreement. It was unthinkable that anyone should so much as entertain a bad thought about our prized playmate, who just three days before, when we children had been down at the stream panning for crawdads, rescued our brother. The towel that we had strung across the little stream to catch hordes of these crustaceans rather than one or two at a time had taken every available hand, leaving our baby brother unattended. We hadn't noticed him, but Teddy, ever mindful of his playmates, had. Suddenly, there was a loud splash; Teddy had jumped into the stream and pushed the little boy back toward shore! Within a matter of months, he would have one more child added to his work load. It was obvious he had come into the world needed by our family, especially us kids . . . especially tonight, with everyone tense and fearful. He tried to interpret Mom's emotions, to see if anything had changed.

"Shhhhh!" responded Mom, her eyes following the ever-so-close red dot.

"It *is* a man!" shrieked my older sister in disbelief upon seeing for herself that the red dot had indeed turned into man.

Responding to his sister's revelation, Kevin cried out in hysteria, "Mama, Red Dot is coming to get us!" Judy jumped up and ran to her younger brother, grabbing his little head with one hand, covering his tiny mouth with the other hand. Tonight she would get away with this action without so much as a peep from him. If she were to do this at any other time, there would be a tattling child crying hysterically.

"You have to be quiet so Red Dot doesn't hear us," Judy said in a gentle voice to her brother, feeling it her obligation to soothe him. Instantly, he stopped crying.

And so it was that Red Dot was named.

Red Dot was now at the mouth of the lane, where house, sheds and barnyards were positioned in a circle on four acres of homestead. The moonlight was bright and we could now see him more clearly. He was tall and slender and wearing faded, tattered jeans and a dark T-shirt with the sleeves rolled up, displaying the entire length of a thin arm and making it obvious to me that Dad was stronger than he was. His jeans rode up over laced-up, high-top boots.

Red Dot dropped his cigarette to the ground and smashed it out with his boot. He looked first in the direction of the house and then to the farm sheds nearby. Next he began walking in the direction of the house. Changing his mind, he turned and walked toward the sheds. Red Dot quickly strolled over to the small machine shed that doubled as the garage for Dad's truck. He peered in the window for a moment and then moved hastily to the door. He reached into his back pocket for a tool, and within moments, the hinge was removed. The cows and their young calves in the yards nearby stood watching, no longer chewing their cuds as they do when content. Discerning the obvious hush that had fallen over the animals, Red Dot raised the arm clutching the hinge and dangling lock, and in mockery, threw them in the direction of the cattle. They hit the fence and fell to the ground with a thud. The seven Canadian wild geese, with their wings clipped so they wouldn't fly away, scattered, honking in protest because their sleep had been disturbed. Their loud cackling started a chain reaction of nervous alert signals from all the animals on the homestead; the ducks started quacking, chickens clucked anxiously, pigs snorted, lambs bleated, mother cows bellowed to their calves and the horses—equally nervous—started striding aimlessly around their pen. The ruckus caused Red Dot to step quickly into the shadow of the gas pump nearby, and the image of his body faded from sight.

He needn't worry tonight; no shots would be fired.

Long moments passed.

Perhaps reassured that no one was home—farm lights had not come on and there was no car in the garage—Red Dot's body language changed from that point on. He no longer walked with a quick step, nor with his flashlight off. He sidled over to the garage and stepped in, irreverently letting the door slam behind him. The beam of his flashlight darted up and down and from side to side on each wall inside, no doubt inventorying what was there. He emerged clutching a strangely shaped gunny sack, the burlap kind issued to farmers when their seed corn and seed beans orders were filled in the spring. Stamped in bold black letters our bags read, "RESERVED FOR BURRES."

Red Dot then ambled over to the large machine shed nearby. There Dad kept his machine tools and machinery that had been purchased second-hand at farm sales or acquired in a trade with a neighbor. After several attempts to break the chain that my father had used to secure the double doors, Red Dot threw his weight into the door, as if his tall and skinny frame could cause it to cave in. It didn't, though a thunderous rolling sound resulted, causing Mom to forcefully yank my sister and me flat to the floor. Teddy stared at Mom as though awaiting his "Sic 'em" to go.

Unperturbed at the renewed choir of noise from the once-again disturbed menagerie of animals, Red Dot took his flashlight and with one quick blow, broke out the window. He walked over to the lumpy burlap seed sack and dumped it out; wrenches and tools clanged as they clamored to the ground. Red Dot then retrieved a bale from the nearby stack of hay, placed the bale beneath the broken window and stepped up on it. He then wrapped his gloved hands with the burlap bag—no doubt to protect himself from the jagged chips of glass that remained in the window sill. With that, he hoisted himself up on the sill, inching his body through the window.

He was in the shed a very long time. When he finally emerged, Red Dot walked to the gas pump, studied its lock carefully, counted off the paces to the underground storage unit that held hundreds of gallons of gas, then disappeared into the head of cattle in the livestock yard. The moon no longer cast a luminescent glow, and it was too dark to follow his path, impossible to see what he was doing.

We were unaware that Red Dot was making his way to the house.

But Teddy knew. Without warning, the dog silently slithered off the porch and crouched in the yard, where he continued to observe the stalker's every move.

"Teddy!" my mother quietly called to the dog. "Get back here!" Tilting his head ever so slightly in the direction of my mother, Teddy looked at her, and because he knew what he needed to do more than she did, he defiantly ignored her order. No one was going to come near his family; he intended to see to it that Red Dot didn't. Within moments, with his belly dragging close to the ground, the dog began to crawl across the length of the yard toward the large wooden sandbox built by my father for his many children. Once there, Teddy crouched beside it and continued his observation in secrecy.

Suddenly there were footsteps on the porch.

In the same instant of our terror, when we realized that Red Dot was on our porch, Teddy began an amazing strategy, obviously intending to lure his family's assailant away from the house and into the yard. First Teddy let out a low belly-wrenching howl, moving his head up and to the side, muffling the sound as if to confuse the location from which it came. It worked. Red Dot, his body now tense, cautiously stepped down from the porch and walked into the yard, as he tried to assess the curious sound he had just heard. It was just what Teddy wanted.

Continuing his ploy to draw the man toward him and away from the house, Teddy then made a series of other weird and unusual sounds. As Red Dot walked toward the noise, Teddy, with his body flat against the ground, backed away from the sandbox and disappeared into the darkness. Red Dot must have felt as though he were hearing things, because he shook his head, seemingly confounded, and then began to approach the house once again. Then, from somewhere in the blackness, Teddy let out the most strange and bloodcurdling sound I've ever heard from an animal.

Startled, Red Dot turned back toward the sound, exploring the darkness of the yard. Obviously afraid, he reached into the burlap bag containing my father's burglarized possessions and pulled out a long shiny metal wrench. He dropped the sack of stolen goods on the ground and walked slowly toward the middle of the yard, holding the wrench in front of him to protect himself from whatever danger lurked there. It was just where Teddy wanted him.

Having circled completely around Red Dot, the dog inched toward the man, slithering silently up behind him. We all watched as our dog, that gentle companion who so patiently allowed us to hug him and ride him and tease him without ever so much as snapping at us or losing his patience, our partner in mischief, our gentle Teddy, now had his teeth bared, his whole body taut and solid. Then he struck.

Teddy threw himself at Red Dot with such force that the man instantly dropped to the ground. Red Dot rolled over and tried to get on his feet. Within an instant, Teddy viciously attacked him again, barking, angry, protecting his family. Swearing profusely now, Red Dot staggered to his feet, his left arm useless as it hung bloody and dangling to his side. Teddy struck again.

But the loving family protector was outgunned by this man, who had little sympathy for four children's best friend. Red Dot raised his hand and with a furious force, struck our magnificent dog in the head with the steel wrench. Crying and yelping in pain, Teddy's body smashed to the ground. Teddy! Our guardian angel was now badly injured.

Still determined to be the victor, Teddy struggled to get up and raged back again, mentally numb to the helplessness of his injured body. Not caring that this magnificent animal was a kindred spirit as well as a warrior, Red Dot hit our pet again and again and again.

"Nooooo!" screamed Judy uncontrollably. "Don't hurt Teddy!"

"He's our doggie, don't hurt our doggie," Mark cried in anguish, tears running down his face. The littlest child screamed and cried because his brother and sisters were. Four children dashed to the door.

Anticipating her children's intentions, Mother rushed to stand guard at the door, trying to stop her children clamoring to get to Teddy's rescue. "Let us out, let us out!" we screamed as Mother momentarily became the enemy as she tried to prevent us from running to help our Teddy. Four children rioted and ran into the yard to rescue our pet and to take care of Teddy the way he had taken care of us so many times.

There was Teddy, now soaked in his own blood, on the ground—Teddy, the dog we loved with so much passion. Now he lay moaning and gasping for air. Slowly, Teddy lifted up his head to get a glimpse of his family, hoping that by now they all had found their way to safety. "It's okay," soothed my sister. "We won't let him hurt you again." Tears streamed from her face down onto the dog. I stroked his broken and bloody body, trying to send him the love and compassion I felt for him and was sure he sensed. He looked at me sadly, and jerked as yet another pain seared through his body. I held him tightly, hoping that my strength would levitate from my body and transfer to his.

But it was too late. The last breath had seeped out from his body; our Teddy didn't move again.

Perhaps because Red Dot heard us screaming and crying and watched as we caressed our dying dog, or maybe because he saw that even as Teddy lay dying, he had turned his head in the direction of the house as if to notify our mother that she must take over from here, Red Dot, too, felt the bond between the dog and his family. I like to think that in those last moments maybe Red Dot felt a touch of remorse over killing such a beautiful animal, an animal justified in attacking him.

Whatever it was, Red Dot slowly limped away, leaving behind the sack of stolen items.

It's hard to comfort children when they have witnessed the devastation of a brutal attack on their pet, especially when the lost pet was as much a part of them as Teddy had been. One by one, we children sought solace in our mother's arms, and were held and rocked there. Too overcome with grief to say anything herself, she pulled us to her body where her unborn baby was protected, knowing that in addition to the loss of Teddy, her children had lost a bit of their innocence as well.

We remembered Teddy for a long time, and included him in our play for almost a year after he was killed. In spirit Teddy joined us children for baseball games, "Catch one for Teddy!" Kevin was fond of saying, as though by mere mention of his name, homage was paid to the dog that had tolerated our antics and loved us so. It was not uncommon for us to "speak" with him as we walked to and from the school bus. From time to time a spanked child could be found sitting on the place of Teddy's grave, complaining and seeking solace, feeling much better for having gone there. And when our newborn brother, Tim, joined the family some months later, we children gathered at Teddy's grave site to introduce the new brother. "Here's our new brother,"

Mark said with tears in his eyes. "He was with us the night you saved our lives, but he just wasn't born yet. So we thought you would want to meet him." He cried as he carried the baby back to the house.

Several years ago my brothers and sisters and I talked about our memories of Teddy, and of this incident. Laurie, of course, had not been born, and Tim was born shortly after Teddy was killed. Kevin, who was three at the time, didn't remember the incident and could recall little about Teddy. Mark's remembrance was mostly about missing the dog's constant companionship and of the horror of the incident in which Teddy was killed. That he could recall in vivid detail.

Judy said she most missed the antics, such as sneaking Teddy into the bedroom window, because she found these acts exciting. Interestingly, she felt that Mom and Dad never did catch on to many of our pranks, while I felt sure they did. I was very sure that Dad knew we often brought Teddy in through the window because of things I watched Dad do. One evening as he was putting us kids down to bed, for example, he stepped on a big fuzzy tail sticking out from under the bed. Mom had just entered the room and I watched as my dad, using his foot, quietly shoved Teddy's tail under the bed, without commenting. He then walked over to Mom and playfully led her from the room, leaving the ritual of our being tucked into bed unfinished.

On another occasion, Dad came into the room before we had a chance to put the screen back on the window. When we heard him coming down the hall, we shoved the screen into the closet, hoping that Dad wouldn't notice the still-open window. Just then, Mom walked in and remarked how cold the room was. Immediately, Dad directed her to get additional blankets. As she left the room, Dad went to our closet, took out the screen and put it back on without saying a word. Of course, we pretended to be either asleep or too sleepy to notice!

Several years ago we asked Dad what he knew. He laughed as he recalled those nights, and admitted being party to Teddy spending the night in our room. Whether or not Mom really knew, I'm not sure. If she did, she didn't let on, because even as we talked about this, she claimed innocence!

A year and a half after Teddy's death, unexpected resolution came.

One Sunday afternoon, a red pickup pulled into our farm-yard. A tall, slender and rather handsome man got out. He came to the house. "I live in Fort Dodge [a town about 15 miles away]," he said. "I was up in the area visiting friends and since I still have one puppy left from a large litter of pups, I thought I might get lucky and find him a home. I thought with your large yard and all, and all these kids, you might be able to give him a good home. He's a really nice little pup, and every child should have a dog, don't you think?"

The man talked fast and looked nervous.

"I have the pup in the truck. If it's okay with you, I'll show him to the kids and see whether they like him." He looked at my father, saw no resistance and hurried to his pickup. Four very excited children followed him. He opened the door of his truck on the passenger side, reached down and picked up a small cardboard box, which he set on the ground beside the truck. Inside was a very small, plump, clean-smelling collie. Within seconds, we were all stroking and petting it, talking to it and arguing over whose turn it was to hold the puppy next. Four hearts were smitten.

With one voice, we all called to our parents. "Can we keep him, please? Please? Please?" We offered all the bargains that children usually do at times like this, eternally swearing to feed and care for the puppy ourselves, to do all our chores, to go to bed without complaining, and a million and one other things designed to soften parents' hearts.

Dad looked the stranger over. "Looks like a nice collie pup; why aren't you selling him? You could probably get quite a bit for a fine dog like that."

We children looked up, terror-stricken that the stranger would change his mind and take the dog away from us. Judy, who was holding the puppy at the time, hugged him so hard he let out a yelp. The stranger smiled at us and pulled out a cigarette. Lighting it, he said, "No, no, you folks would be doing me a favor, put my mind at rest if you'd take the dog. I just want him to have a good home. And like I said, kids should have a dog. Lotta love between kids and dogs, you know. It looks like they like him alright."

Mom and Dad exchanged glances, but it was clear that they had already given in. "Okay, Mister, and thanks. It looks as if the kids have a new dog. Since he's just a pup, guess we'd better take his box, too."

I ran back to retrieve the box. That's when I noticed it. There in the box was a rumpled burlap bag . . . marked "RESERVED FOR BURRES."

Red Dot had come back to repay a debt.

5 Coffee for Four

I grew up in Iowa. Folks there are fond of saying that Iowa is God's country. In some ways it is; the land is rich, and luscious vegetation and abundant crops sprout from the earth on cue. Hardy and chemical-free animals with gentle eyes graze in sweet-smelling meadows. Farmers tend to their animals as do the 4-H youth—kindly and with great care. Sometimes it's difficult to distinguish livestock from pets.

Iowans are often referred to as the salt of the earth and the backbone of America, and justifiably so. To them, the practice of what is commonly known as barn-raising—in which everyone pitches in to help a neighbor in need—is second nature. Helping out your fellow traveler is just what you do, as was witnessed again when everyone—young, old and in-between—turned out to help friends, neighbors and total strangers recover from the recent flooding in the Midwest.

Iowa's four distinct seasons are full of enormous and awesome beauty. Lush green springtimes promise the likes of purple and white lilacs, magnificent daffodils, the biggest tiger lilies you have ever seen and the tiniest purple flowers, no bigger than your little fingernail, inside of which—as any grandma will tell you—sits the king on his throne. These and an assortment of other gorgeous and breathtaking flowers add their intoxicating fragrance to the fresh spring air. Summers are lazy and warm, filled with the squeals of kids' water fights and barbecues you can smell for miles, served on homemade picnic tables that can comfortably seat three families—which they usually do. Nearly every house has a porch, and in the summer, well-used swings hang on those porches, scarred with the initials of generations of owners. Fall for sure is God's idea of a lavish art festival; and winter—it's Iowa where the term "winter wonderland" originated.

I spent my first two decades of life in Iowa. I know Iowa's springs are wet, summers are humid, falls cold, and winters—well, winters are why I live in sunny southern California now! But Iowa is not without my heart. My brothers and sisters live there, as do my parents—two of the most exemplary people I have ever known. Because my parents and I live so far apart, we often miss each other, especially around the holidays. So every year they beg me to come back, especially at Christmas time, and every year I do what every good Iowa farm girl now living in sunny southern California would do: I send them airline tickets to come spend a few weeks with me!

And each year they do. Each year I am warmed and nourished by the family connections we share, by the memories we recall and talk about again and again. Always I am amazed by the encompassing love my parents share and by the appreciation and respect they have for each other. I am so very happy to see them come, and so thankful that we have another year to talk about and to listen to each other's stories of those things that bring meaning and purpose to our lives; what we are doing and how we are faring with each of the challenges put to us, or as my mother says, "our crosses to bear." Ever mindful of old Father Time, I try to make their stay as joyful as I can. One big treat is for them to take over my master bedroom. This glorious room sprawls the entire second floor of my lodge, and with a fireplace, sunken tub and view of the Pacific Ocean overlooking 100 acres of wildlife preserve, it's a very comfortable place to be! For them, I give it up willingly.

Because my closet is next to the bedroom, in the early mornings I often sneak upstairs and get dressed in the nearby walk-in closet, and then slip out without their knowing it. This has been the pattern for several years now, and no one seems to mind my laziness about not transferring my clothes ahead of time to a downstairs closet. If they do notice, they don't let on. My sense is that they are fully aware of what is going on and feel good that I am convenienced by leaving my clothes in the master closet, and that it relieves them of any guilt they may feel for my moment of inconvenience.

Yesterday seemed like just another of those days, quickly and quietly getting dressed in the dark of my closet—until I began my descent down the spiral staircase. There I witnessed such a touching scene between my parents that I couldn't help but watch, even though I felt like an intruder, as though I had no right to their private and personal moment.

What added intrigue was how unusual the circumstance was. My mother is a morning person. She is up at the crack of dawn—

somewhere around "o'dark thirty." She likes this time alone. First things first, she brews a pot of coffee and then gathers her reading materials. If you are looking for Mother in the early morning hours, you'll find her on the patio next to any shrub or flower in bloom. If you can't find her it's because she is taking a walk. She says she enjoys talking with her boss—communing with God—before the rush hour begins. This morning was no different.

My dad, because he is a farmer, sometimes gets in from the fields or from chores around midnight. In the harsh of winter weather, he often has to make midnight and early morning rounds to make sure that any newborn animals are taken in to be warmed up so they don't freeze to death. He is *not* a morning person. As children, all six kids would gather in the hall outside the kitchen to draw straws to decide whose turn it was to be the first to approach Dad to see if he were anywhere near human. Having chosen the shortest straw more than a time or two, I can tell you that not only is Dad definitely not a morning person; the first half-hour when he is up, he is unapproachable! For some reason, he was up early this morning.

When I was upstairs I hadn't noticed whether or not my dad was still in bed. I assumed he was. But here were my two parents already awake. I saw each coming from a different room, moving toward each other.

I can only assume what led up to this moment. Apparently my mother, while sitting in the backyard, had glanced up at the upstairs window and noticed that my father was awake and decided to get two cups of coffee and take them upstairs. Unbeknownst to her, my father probably had the same thing in mind. He must have looked out the window from the second floor and, seeing her in the backyard, gone down to get them coffee. Probably when he noticed that she was no longer in the yard, he assumed she had returned to the master bedroom to get dressed. He would take the coffee upstairs.

My father is curious and a wanderer; nothing escapes his watchful eyes. Holding two cups of coffee in one hand, he stopped to examine the browning leaf of a nearby house plant. First he looked at the top side of the leaf, and then with a finger much thicker than I remembered from childhood, flicked the leaf up to observe the underside as well. I looked to the other side of the circular divide, and observed my mother as she came into view—a beautiful woman with graying hair wearing that darn old bathrobe my father gave her for Mother's Day nearly 20 years ago, walking ever so gently, balancing two full cups of coffee, one for her, and one for the man she has passionately loved for a lifetime. I glanced back at my father, wondering when they would discover each other. Obviously now satisfied with the leaf, my father continued his journey. There he was, this still handsome, gray-haired man, carrying two cups of steaming coffee, the small china cups dwarfed in those big, weathered hands. He still growls sometimes, but not when it comes to this woman he loves. And so they moved closer to each other, each totally unaware of the actions of the other, oblivious to the fact that they had each fetched coffee for the other, unknowing that they were about to meet. They slowly inched toward each other. Amused, I watched silently.

As they neared the end of the circular hall that divides three rooms, they discovered the presence of the other. They stood still for a moment, these two lovers, and looked at each other and smiled tenderly, then sheepishly. Within seconds, their eyes glanced to the coffee each poured for the other, and realizing the humor in four cups of coffee between them, they laughed gleefully. Their eyes met once again, and as though it were a well-rehearsed script, in unison they stooped down and set four cups of coffee on the floor, and moved into each other's arms, embracing tenderly, lingering in the moment as lovers do. They belonged to each other. Each knew it, honored it and felt honored in being loved so completely by the other. Good times, tough times, all times—very early on they had vowed they would spend their lives together. And meant it. Two separate energies formed a third force, transforming two distinct personalities into one heart. Their love was magic, energizing.

Quietly, I sat down in the stairwell; it wasn't right to trespass into their moment any longer.

In education we like to say there are "teachable moments." Some of the most transforming moments in my life come from glimpses into the lives of these two extraordinary people. They are in their early seventies, so they are no strangers to each other; they have been married nearly 50 years. All relationships take a great deal of work, including good ones in keeping them that way. Surely the history of my parents' love carries many hardships just as it does joy. But their commitment to nourish their love and hold their relationship sacred, their willingness to be open to each other's love even as it changes over the years, their dedication to creating a healthy and durable union, the appreciation each feels in being the recipient of the other's kindness, the honor each feels to be "of service" to the other, the respect each bestows upon the other—and all the work it entails—may just hold a few answers for those who, in today's times of seeming impermanence, are trying to understand love and believe that it can be permanent.

As I watch my parents, I see the potency of a love truly shared, and the spectrum of difficulties it can transform.

6

Member of the Gang

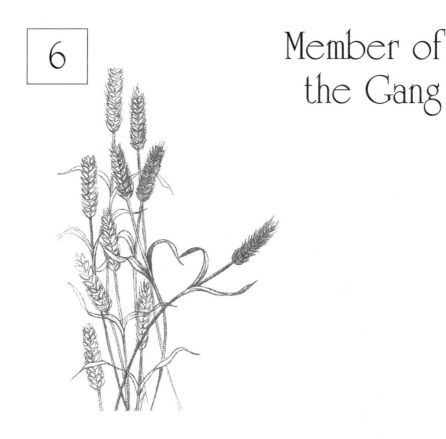

"What a fraidy-cat," my sister, Judy, taunted. "All you have to do is run over there, pick it up and run back. How difficult can this be for goodness sakes! I've shown you how to do it ten times now. It's simple, there's nothing to it, and besides, you know it's *your* turn. I've taken my turn four weeks in a row now, and since your birthday comes *after* mine, you *have* to go next. Besides," she added, resorting to scare tactics, "if you don't go, we are going to vote you out of the Gang!" Four younger club members looked first at their leader and then at me, no doubt thanking God that my birth had preceded theirs.

Being voted out of the club was definitely a legitimate threat! When you were on the outs with my sister, you were in for some *bad* times. Judy had a knack for doling out stiff penalties; she was extraordinarily gifted at making alienation seem like a prison sentence. Besides that, I had just been granted some goodies I didn't want taken away, so I was really at risk here.

Hadn't she let me sit with her and her crowd this past Friday at school during lunch? Hadn't she let me read the note bad-girl Marilyn Johnson had written describing her petting session with Stuart Stockdale?

And when Marilyn became upset because Judy shared it with me, hadn't my sister admirably defended her actions by saying it was okay because I was *her* sister?

Judy had even come to my rescue when Tommy James told everyone I had kissed him, a terrible and embarrassing reputation-ruining lie.

And hadn't she sided with me against that smart-aleck Dennis Christiansen's verbal assaults on the bus? This big bruiser had a penchant for teasing and name-calling, and being subjected to his ego could be brutal. Dennis was a handsome guy with cool clothes, pumped-up muscles and a fast mouth. Everyone at school both idolized and feared him. It didn't matter that he was older than my sister; whatever Dennis said, Judy would dish back worse than what he offered up. My sister did not fear anyone! No, I simply could not gamble with losing my sister's approval, no matter how scared I was at taking my turn. I would do what I had to do. I was not about to chance being voted out of the club.

And so like any other young kid allowing herself to be coerced into subversive activity, I darted to the delivery truck some 300 meters away. The goal was simple: get to the van, grab one or more items, then dash back to the Gang's headquarters without getting caught! Some items were more desirable than others: chocolate ice cream was worth three points, strawberry flavor was worth two points and vanilla, one point; Brach's butterscotch candies were worth two points, and sugar-wafer cookies (three-color flavor worth five points, three points for chocolate, vanilla worth one point) were liked by all, particularly our leader.

This game, the latest of many, was invented by my sister herself. "The objective," she would say, "is to show that you are worthy of *being members*." Judy hadn't yet learned about participatory management; her rule was somewhere between Eva Peron and Atilla the Hun, her leadership style somewhere between dictatorship and sole proprietorship. She elected herself leader and appointed us members. Our motto, "We're not a club, we're a gang!" was made up by Judy and presented to us for a vote. That's just the way things worked. Judy decided on the activity we were going to get involved in and presented it to us for a vote. Of course, no alternatives were ever presented. We met every Sunday immediately following the ritual of Sunday school and the family noon feast and cleanup, convening the moment our parents locked us out of the house for some private time. Judy liked to keep these meetings short, so we dispensed with time-consuming things like asking questions and having discussions. Judy's dictates were final. Five gang members—Bettie, Mark, Kevin, Tim and Laurie—were loyal subjects to their older sister.

Too frightened to actually step foot inside the truck (Judy was a very discriminating thief and would go inside and carefully select the goods that would qualify for her heist), and scared to death of getting caught red-handed, I stood outside the opened sliding door of the van, and with my eyes peeled in the direction of Great Auntie's house, grabbed the first thing that my hand touched. Feeling successful in my robbery, I ran back to the hideout where the rest of the posse awaited my return.

"Bread! No way! You dumb kid, you damn got a loaf of white bread," Judy laughed, holding it up for all to see. Her laughter stopped abruptly and with great scorn on her face she yelled, "What are we going to do with a loaf of bread?" Mocking my catch in front of the other members was definitely not very good for building self-esteem, but she wasn't into that sort of thing. I secretly wished I had been born first and then I could say these things to her and she would have to put up with it. Better yet, I wished I had been born an only child. As though I had not already been berated enough, she added, "Can't you do anything right? Get out there and do it right this time, you stupid fool." With that she opened the door to the pump shed, our sacred little hiding spot, and pushed me into the wide open yard. For added effect, she grabbed the door and slammed it shut behind me. She really had a way with drama.

Without questioning her authority, I darted back to the truck to make another hit. I had been both coached and warned that this had better be "successful." Knowing that the delivery man would be leaving Great Auntie's house at any minute, and even more fearful of getting caught, I once again kept my eyes peeled on the screen door to Great Auntie's house, still too frightened to actually enter the truck. I reached my hand into the truck, and flopping it around until I felt something that wasn't bread-like, I grabbed another item. Panting and with heart pounding, I ran with my new acquisition back to the hideout. Once more, I lay my catch before the gang's Queen.

"Good Lord!" my sister roared as she looked at what my heist had reaped. "Look what that idiot retrieved this time!" She held up a plastic bag that contained a pair of yellow rubber gloves, the kind those fancy ladies on television wore when they were doing dishes. Like a good manager keeping track of our progress, Judy graphed and plotted the results of the trips to the delivery van on the badly worn sheet of paper tacked to the wall of the shed. In the column under my name she wrote, 'dumb bread, stupid gloves.'

"You are one dumb kid, and useless to the club," she said, going for maximum embarrassment. She was a master at ridicule, too. Pausing just long enough to build suspense, she announced, "I say you're out!" She grabbed the bag of rubber gloves and flicked them over her shoulder, hitting Shep, the family dog and Gang's mascot, in the head. Shep had been lying in the corner, observing our every move. He kept his eyes on Judy; he, too, knew that whatever the next action was, it would be initiated by her.

"Hey, wait a minute!" I countered. "How was I supposed to know that truck carried something other than food? And didn't I prove that I took my turn? It's not fair that I'm out of the club. Let's vote on it." I looked to the other members, all younger than I, for support. Watching Judy's dominion over me had given them a pretty good theoretical understanding of hierarchy, pecking order and other forms of oppression—at least enough to know they had little to no clout with this dominant force. Their eyes instantly turned from me to Judy. Perhaps swayed by the ballot of pity and distress on their faces, she voted on behalf of all of us and said, "Okay, you can stay in the club under *one* condition. You have to take another turn for the next two weeks, but you better do better. If you don't, you will be out for good!" My sentence had been levied; I had been found only *half* guilty.

And so began my membership in the the Gang, made up of six kids, all of us brothers and sisters. My older sister Judy had crowned herself Queen and King, all in one. Bold, gutsy and colorful, this budding adolescent could and would take on many a challenge, from standing up to my father—the ultimate sign of omnipotence and machismo—to out-foxing old Mr. Samuels, the driver of the vending truck, whose fate it was on every Saturday to become an innocent victim to our Gang's hold-up.

Great Auntie Hilda was my father's aunt. Her house sat about 20 rods from our home, both places nestled deep within 40 acres of picturesque homestead. Hers was a majestic old mansion built in the mid-1800s, a house with nine bedrooms. Great Auntie had outlived her numerous brothers and sisters, her childhood friends and a great many of her relatives, for that matter. Still in good health at 92, she was vigorous and as sharp as a tack.

A grand old dame and wealthy, too, Great Auntie took pride in the fact that she could afford to have groceries delivered to her house by way of the traveling vendor. She justified this extravagant measure by saying she didn't want to inconvenience others by asking them to take her into town. Frankly, I think the delivery truck was a premeditated scheme, a strategy to manipulate us kids. When you live on the same farm as your nephew, his wife and six children, you need to carve out a role for yourself and assign it the status you need. Great Auntie did this by fashioning herself a grandmother of sorts to my brothers and sisters and me. She assigned herself the duty of ordering us around. But first she spoiled us. She was one savvy old lady.

At 92, she also needed bargaining power. A supply of ice cream and cookies became easy bribes for kids when she wanted us to mow the lawn, fetch the mail down the long lane, replenish the supply of cobs for the pot-bellied stove or refill the coal bin in the basement. Great Auntie Hilda could hold her own with the six of us—in fact, the odds were in her favor!

The delivery truck arrived without fail every Saturday, right around noon, and coincided with the rise of Great Auntie's popularity with us. From about noon on Saturday and for the rest of the day, we could be bribed, bought and enslaved. No doubt Great Auntie was aware of her transitory popularity, too, since it was on Saturday that she presented each of us with a list of things she wanted us to do for her. We did these chores gladly. Great Auntie rewarded us with generous amounts of sweets.

Unfortunately for Great Auntie, there were drawbacks to using this approach with us. Should she stand on the porch and shout to us on any other day, we pretended not to hear. I used to feel badly when Great Auntie stood on the steps and called out our names, hoping to catch one of us in order to have us bring her more cobs or coal. If we were in the presence of Judy, the sound of Great Auntie's voice would mean we all ran for cover. We did this as much for Judy as anyone else. Ever so unsympathetic, my sister cajoled, "Why bother; she has no ice cream or cookies left. Hold out until Saturday, and it'll be worth your time! No one is to answer her in the middle of the week. If anyone betrays the rules," she warned, "then that person is *out!*"

I think Great Auntie was wise to this, too, because on several occasions I saw her open the door, and upon catching a glimpse of my sister, Great Auntie quickly closed it. She took to leaving an empty five-gallon pail on the porch when she needed cobs, and the coal bucket when she needed coal. From time to time, the empty pails would mysteriously get filled. Sometimes I hurried and filled the bucket for her without being seen by my sister, as would Mark, the most humane of all of us. But neither of us did this if my sister was around. It was no fun to be caught between the power plays of Great Auntie and our leader.

This heist-without-getting-caught game went on for nearly three months. On one particularly beautiful spring Saturday,

Great Auntie gathered us all around. She informed us that today's To-Do list was not like other Saturdays; this was going to be an extra big spring cleanup day. Judy would be needed for five hours, I would be needed for three-and-a-half hours, Mark and Kevin would be needed for three hours. Tim could help anyone he wanted, though his real responsibility was to watch Laurie who, at just three years old, was more hindrance than help. It was decided that she could hang around anyway, as could the canine member of the family. Great Auntie knew we were all inseparable, and the dog went wherever his kids went. Shep was a valuable commodity and he knew it. If Shep wasn't in demand to console a youngster who had taken a bad spill on a bicycle or was recovering from a spanking, he was needed to catch some silly object thrown at him to fetch. Sometimes he became the third base for a game of baseball and sometimes a scapegoat for a child's frustration. He didn't mind. He gladly offered up his body for use and abuse, whether a child needed it for hugs or warmth, or grabbed onto him, snatching a ride on his back. It was hard work belonging to this motley crew, and he loved every minute of it. Shep was right there in the lineup.

We greeted the announcement of our work schedule like children with terrible toothaches agreeing to go to the dentist— groaning, but with a sense of gratitude. While the amount of work seemed enormous, we were also anticipating enormous rewards. After all, we were used to being well-rewarded for our Saturday work.

Having been the oldest of nine children herself and chiefly responsible for caring for them, Great Auntie was no novice when it came to motivating others. She spared nothing now. Using five-star motivational techniques that would win points with Lee Iacocca, she began by stating the wonderful outcomes for accomplishing all these tasks. These included the possibility of finding some old toy or keepsake in the attic clean-up, enjoying the sight and smell of the roses we would be planting when they bloomed in the not too distant future, and feeling proud when others—the bus driver and kids on the bus, for instance—miraculously remarked how nicely groomed the yards looked. When we rolled our eyes on that one, she glanced over at the dish of cookies sitting on the tabletop nearby. Having enlisted our support once again, Great Auntie told us where each body would be stationed for his or her assigned work. And finally, to set the stage for this production, this wise old manager added a final gesture to lure our *full* participation. She had choreographed the whole thing by setting four paper sacks on the table.

And so six children undertook a most arduous day of work, with great anticipation of the big pay-off.

Finally, after what seemed like the longest day of our lives, the work was done. Great Auntie led six dirty and tired children into her huge kitchen. We sat on the stained-wood floor, awaiting our promised rewards.

Great Auntie knew how to milk the situation. She slowly walked to the refrigerator, then stood there for a second. She turned and smiled at us, no doubt sensing our excitement. Great Auntie opened the door, pulled out something with both hands and shut the refrigerator door with her foot. She put her hands behind her back; it was obvious she had one treat in each hand. She walked toward the youngest kids and smiling, told each child to choose the hand they wanted. When they did, each was handed a Popsicle—a complete Popsicle, mind you, a two-part one, not just the half-a-Popsicle we were accustomed to. The older children exchanged glances, almost drooling in anticipation. This was going to be great!

With four other children watching in obvious expectancy of what awaited them, Great Auntie leaned on her fancy cane and taking her time, methodically told Tim and Laurie what a wonderful job they had done, an act that was totally devoid of meaning for them. Oblivious to her, they licked away on their treats, chatting and being silly with each other. They were too young and unworldly to know this lowly payoff was below minimum wage, and so were ecstatic with their treats. No doubt Great Auntie was aware of this, but she painstakingly continued with her oration.

Next she singled out Mark, the oldest boy, leaving Kevin, the middle boy, to wait his turn at being called. Mark was praised, given a bag of chocolate chip cookies and dismissed. Used to rewards and punishments given out in order of hierarchy, he seemed a bit confounded that he should have his turn before Kevin, but gladly accepted his treat and praise. He went outside and sat on the step waiting for the rest of his gang.

The three remaining children sat in total silence, now perplexed and quite unsure of Great Auntie's incentive plan. Finally she walked over to the table and handed both Kevin and me one sack, and two sacks to Judy. We were directed to open them. With great anticipation, we tore open the bags. Inside my bag were the following:

> *a dilapidated empty strawberry ice cream box*
> *three empty packages of sugar wafer cookies*
> *two empty jars of marshmallow creme*
> *an empty bag of white bread*
> *a package of yellow rubber gloves.*

Just when I thought there was nothing more, I noticed a wrinkled, dirty piece of paper. It was Judy's itemized list of things I had personally been responsible for taking from the delivery van over the past three months! (You can only imagine what was in Judy's bag.) In Great Auntie's neat printing down the side of the list was a tally of the dollar amount of the goods.

My heart started beating very fast and it took me a minute to figure out what was happening. I looked up at Great Auntie. Her face no longer smiled. Slowly she handed me one more piece of paper. It was a list of how many hours of work it would take for me to pay off the debt. She then pulled a small chiseled pencil she had stuck into her hair and supported by her ear and, as three children watched in shock, she wrote, "Paid in Full" on each of our lists.

We sat there, too horrified to speak, now all too willing to be subjected to the obligatory lectures that we knew we were about to receive.

"We promise never to do this again," stammered my sister Judy.

"Oh, please don't tell Mom and Dad," Kevin stuttered.

I was still in shock, and so said nothing.

Great Auntie looked at three very scared and sincerely sorry children. "I'm happy that you have learned a lesson," she said. "I trust this sort of thing will never happen again."

"Oh, Great Auntie," Judy said, with the proper amount of remorse in her voice. "We promise never to do it again." And then, glancing at the piece of paper she was clutching in her hands, she hastily added, "And we promise to fill your coal and cob pails whenever you need them."

Knowing that we were all truly remorseful, Great Auntie said, "That will be very nice." And then she quietly added, "You may go."

And we did.

7

The Pheasant

Growing up on a farm provided a daily opportunity to see how mankind and nature are interrelated. Both of my parents had a supreme sense of respect for Mother Nature and everything in her realm. This was demonstrated time and time again in my childhood, and was personified by the events of one particularly memorable day in early spring.

The bright sun filtered through the clouds, warming the fields of alfalfa that my father was mowing. Within a day or two it would be put into bales of hay, gathered from the field, stored in the hay loft and used to feed our livestock. I stood at the fence line with the lunch my mother had prepared for my father, watching as he cautiously guided the tractor up and down the field, head down, eyes closely observing the movements of the mower. As he neared the end of the field, Dad saw me holding out the lunch for him. He stopped and motioned that it was safe for me to bring it to him.

"Please, Daddy, take me for a ride," I begged as he ate his lunch. I loved riding on the tractor with my father. It was quite a treat because children were forbidden from riding it alone; it was for grown-ups only. Extremely safety-conscious, Dad rarely allowed us children to even be near it, let alone climb up on this big "dangerous" machine. So protective was he of his family, he seldom asked my mother to drive the tractor even short distances—such as to fuel it—around the farmstead.

I also liked riding on the tractor because I relished the feel of the wind blowing through my hair and the warm sun on my face, arms and legs. But most of all, I loved being close to my father; sitting near him on the tractor seat inside his protective arms was a very loving feeling, and I adored my daddy and everything about him. I found his high energy and love for the outdoors contagious; his charisma exciting; and his running commentary about everything around him interesting—nothing escaped his eyes: birds, bees, flowers, clouds, passing cars and trucks. All became fodder for a comment, story or lesson.

"Please, Daddy, can't I ride with you?" I asked again.

"No, no. It's not safe for you to be on the open tractor; I never know when the long sharp sickle of the mower will come dangerously close to a nesting pheasant or a rabbit or a fox. When that happens, I have to stop suddenly and that could cause you to fall. No, I'll give you a ride another time."

"Oh, please, Daddy. I'll be so careful. I'll stay out of your way. Take me with you for a little ways, and then I'll get off and I won't complain even if it's a long way home."

It never took too much begging with my father. When his children wanted to be with him, he was a soft touch.

I sat on the edge of the tractor seat between my father's legs, holding on to his knees, trying as hard as I could not to get in his way as he constantly shifted from side to side. With the skill of a surgeon, Dad began by first looking ahead as he aligned the tractor with the meticulously straight line of still-standing alfalfa—a sharp contrast to the stems, cut off from their life source by the mower, now lying flat against the ground. After he did this he shifted to look behind, continuously observing the long row of the razor-sharp sickle blade as it deftly sliced millions of hearty alfalfa stalks the instant it came into contact with them. One powerful arm steered the tractor while the other arm wrapped around his 10-year-old daughter, protecting her in its grip.

Suddenly a pheasant squawked and jerked skyward, and in the same instant my father instinctively stepped on the clutch. As the tractor lurched to a halt, my father flung both his arms around me, stopping me from being thrown into the steering wheel or off the tractor.

Protecting me had made it impossible to save the female pheasant minding her nest. As quickly and sharply as she rose into the sky, she fell from it, hitting the ground with a deadening thump, then violently and aimlessly thrashing around. Both her legs had been severed near her body.

"Oh, no," my father said softly, getting down from the tractor and lifting me off with him. He hurried over to the wounded bird, picked her up and, with tears in his eyes, stroked her beautiful sleek feathers, apologizing to her for the pain he had caused.

He shook his head and said in a voice that housed as much disgust as it did passion, "She can never live this way." He was talking as much to the universe as he was to me. "She'll be easy prey to any predator," he added, and in his next breath, he took hers. With one quick flick of my father's wrist, she no longer had to contemplate her fate in the wild.

He flung the head of the now-decapitated bird far away from us. Then gently pulling the bird's wings together, he held her upside down so that her blood would drain from her body and not be absorbed into the meat, which would have made it inedible.

Over the years I had often experienced the killing of fowl: chickens, turkeys, geese and ducks all made their way to our table in a similar fashion. I was saddened as much by my father's sense of devastation as from having witnessed the bird's death.

Dad gathered up the three orphaned eggs from the pheasant's nest, which now lay in disarray, and placed them in the empty lunch box that sat alongside the pheasant, and home we went.

My mother prepared the pheasant for dinner that evening. At the supper table, my father talked about the nature of Mother Nature, and our role in protecting and comforting all her creatures. His sadness had been replaced by his appreciation for such an excellent dinner and the safety of family at his side.

We children were taken by surprise. We had come to the table fully prepared to mourn alongside our father. I had shared with all my brothers and sisters the sequence of events and Dad's reaction: we felt sad for him as well as the pheasant. But our father wasn't sad at all; in fact, he seemed jubilant. We children didn't understand his changed mood. After all, we were all still a bit sad—and not at all sure if we were going to take a helping of the roast pheasant now nestled in the glass baking dish.

"Daddy, why didn't we let the pheasant live?" my sister Judy inquired. "She could still sit on her eggs and hatch them, even without legs."

"Without legs," Dad answered, "the mother pheasant would no longer be able to teach her chicks to hunt after they hatched. And worse, without legs, she couldn't protect herself against predators like the fox. No, I'm afraid she wouldn't make it out there without legs."

Always the humanitarian, my brother Mark chided, "Daddy, no one, not even a hungry old fox, would hurt a poor pheasant who didn't have legs."

"Legs or no legs," responded my father, "a fox will eat a pheasant any day, any time of day."

"That's not very nice," cried my littlest brother.

"Why?" I questioned. "Why would a fox want a wounded bird?"

"Because," replied my father, "it's in his nature."

We all looked curious and confounded. Sensing that he had not been completely understood, our father leaned forward, rested both elbows on the table and, with his best storytelling voice and most animated face, began his yarn. "Once upon a time, there was a pheasant who, while out foraging for food, broke both her wings. And since her wings were broken, she couldn't fly. Now this was a real big problem because her home was on the other side of the lake, and she wanted to get there. She stood by the edge of the lake thinking what to do. She flapped and flapped her wings, but it was no use; she was too injured to fly.

"Along came a fox who, seeing the pheasant's problem, said, 'Looks like you have a problem. What's the matter?'

'Oh,' said the pheasant, 'I live on the other side of the lake and I've broken my wings and now I can't fly home.'

'What a coincidence!' said the fox. 'I live on the other side of the lake, too, and I'm on my way home. Why don't you hop on my back and I'll give you a ride.'

'But you're a fox and you will eat me,' said the pheasant.

'No, no,' said the fox. 'Don't be afraid. Hop on. I'll take you home.'

"So the pheasant, anxious to get home, hopped on the fox's back and he began the swim home. But just before they reached the shore on the other side of the lake, the fox shook the pheasant from his back, causing her to fall into the water. Frightened, the pheasant cried out, 'Oh, please don't eat me.'

'I'm afraid I have to,' said the fox.

'But why?' pleaded the pheasant.

" 'Because,' grinned the fox, 'it's in my nature.'"

With differing degrees of understanding—and deep in thought—we children quietly began eating, absorbing the visions of the story we had just heard. And so it was the taste of pheasant was made delicious to me—and became symbolic of the nature of Mother Nature and of my father's understanding and respect for it.

The pheasant's three eggs were given to a plump old goose who dutifully sat on the eggs around the clock, getting up from the nest only briefly to eat and to turn the eggs. Within weeks, three pheasant chicks emerged. After several weeks of caretaking, we released them into the wild, making the cycle complete: my father had taken from Mother Nature and given back to her as well. In making the exchange, he taught us a bit more about the nature of Mother Nature and our role in protecting and comforting those in it. And to hold her in the highest regard—as much as we did our father.

8

The
Letter(less)
Sweater

"Going steady" was pretty heady stuff in junior high school. This ceremonial dance followed a simple pattern: a boy asked a girl to wear his athletic letter sweater, she accepted, and then she wore it as often as possible around school. This envied exhibition showcased for everyone that you were desired by the opposite sex—and probably getting kissed—so there was a great deal of eminence associated with this ritual for both boys and girls. Of course, it put quite a bit of pressure on the boys to earn the coveted letter sweater. This is the reason so many boys went out for sports—it was the only way you could possess one of those status-laden tokens, a prerequisite if you were to become "somebody." It was also an essential ingredient if you wanted to go steady with a girl who had already gained a considerable amount of rank and clout because she was considered popular. To be popular *and* in possession of a letter sweater was really something; it expanded a girl's already distinctive reputation to darn near nobility.

Of course, if you broke up you had to give the sweater back, which ultimately gave the girl a lot of power in the relationship. When Sue Goodell broke up with Jeff Lundgren, she wouldn't return his sweater because she knew that Jeff wanted to give it to Mary Duran. Breaking up could be tricky, too.

While going steady offered mystery and intrigue, if the boy didn't possess a letter sweater, your reputation wasn't much above that of your average run-of-the-mill kid. The letter sweater was the thing.

I was really a nobody. I not only wasn't going steady with a guy who had a letter sweater, I didn't even have a boyfriend. This presented me with a real problem when several of my friends and I got the idea to try out for cheerleading. When you tried out for cheerleading, you had to wear a guy's letter sweater up there on stage. Besides being the custom, it was part of the costume. It showed school spirit and advertised that you were tethered to a boy who was an athlete. In other words, you were a *real* somebody.

Cheerleading tryouts were held in early spring. By this time of the year, nearly every boy with a letter sweater had found a girl who was willing to wear his. In the event you didn't have a boyfriend and intended to try out for cheerleading, you needed to find a boy who was still in possession of his sweater—and willing to lend it to you. Or you had to ask a girl who wasn't trying out if she would lend you her boyfriend's sweater. All of this got to be very complicated and was in and of itself a test of self-esteem. I needed to round up a letter sweater to wear for tryouts and began asking around. Everyone, it seemed, was going steady or had loaned out their letter sweaters to one of the many girls trying out for cheerleading. One day, to my surprise—and relief—a newly cleaned and pressed sweater folded carefully in a box directly from the cleaners had been placed in my locker. Someone had come to my rescue. I was thrilled.

Nothing was more of a social event than when the entire school gathered in the auditorium to vote for the chosen six, those girls who would win the coveted title of "cheerleader." Winning this pageant was quite an honor. If being an athlete and having a letter sweater gave ultimate status to a boy, being selected as a cheerleader brought maximum status to a girl. And the day this was determined was the day of reckoning. All the contestants were anxious. We all wanted to win a coveted spot on next year's squad.

For moral support, each girl sat with her group of friends—all of us scattered throughout the auditorium. When the physical education teacher, who was always in charge of the cheerleading events, called out the numbers assigned to each group of girls trying out, you got up and headed toward the stage. If you were lucky, your little group of friends applauded and stomped their feet (very loudly, hopefully)—anything to let the rest of the auditorium know that you had groupies. There was an unmistakable association between the amount of noise made for each contestant and those girls who won.

We were group number seven. When the teacher called out for our group to go up on stage, my friends pushed me out of my seat and I nervously headed for the stage. I climbed up the three steps, anxious every step of the way, and took my place in the middle; there was to be a girl on each side of me. A girl in the front row let out a gasp. "Oh my God, she's wearing Alan Thompson's sweater!"

Alan was the school nerd. Quite simply, he was just too nice a guy. And too smart. Unfortunately, no one told him that in junior high it wasn't smart to be nice, or nice to be smart. So he was unanimously selected to be the school nerd. Alan looked the part. He had thick black curly hair and had a bad hair day every day. He really did wear thick glasses, and somewhere in his elementary school years his brain had advanced to college-level studies. Plus, he walked like a duck. Poor Alan. He could do *nothing* to change things. Worse, everyone knew that because Alan had been the team's water boy and overall gofer for three years, the coach had given him a sweater (without the letter) as a token of appreciation, making his sweater less than desirable to all.

I stood there for a moment, watching and waiting for the other two wannabes to join me. It was soon apparent that no one else was coming.

At first I thought that maybe I had heard wrong and had gone up on stage too soon. Perhaps the teacher had called eleven and not seven; the groups weren't necessarily called in order. Terrified, I stood there alone in the middle of the big auditorium's stage in front of every one of my schoolmates. And in Alan-the-Nerd's letterless sweater!

Assuming I was a one-act show, the physical education teacher called out, "You may begin now." A dead silence fell over the auditorium as they all watched me, wondering what I was going to do. I was so mortified that my feet would not take me off stage, and with suicide unacceptable at the Evangelical Lutheran Church I attended, I had no choice but to do the cheer alone.

You have no idea what it's like to do—*totally alone*—a cheer that requires three able bodies. Nor can you get a feel for the humiliation I suffered being on a stage alone in front of my peers in Alan-the-Untouchable's letterless sweater. Obviously once the other two girls saw me going up in Alan's sweater, they backed out. Seems I had committed the unpardonable sin; I had touched Alan's sweater, and they would have rather died than be on the same stage with *that* sweater—the one without the scarlet letter!

How was I to know that everyone would recognize the sweater as belonging to Alan?

I didn't get voted to be cheerleader, but I did make runner-up. In other words, should a cheerleader DIE from yelling cheers, I would fill the vacated slot.

Twenty years had only slightly diminished the twinge of embarrassment I felt at having been a part of ridiculing Alan. Because of this I made a point of contacting Alan in recent years to ask him how he had experienced those years, and in particular, *that* notorious event. True to his style of being unfazed by life's little challenges, he laughed and said confidently, "Oh, it was no big thing, really. That was a very good year for me. All my dreams came true. Especially the two most important ones. I wanted an athletic sweater and I wanted you to wear it. So when I found out that you needed a sweater to wear at the tryouts, well, my dream came true. There you were, up front and center stage in front of all the other students wearing my sweater. It was perfect! I was so proud. That was a great day for me . . . much better than yours, I trust!"

Alan hadn't experienced humiliation at all. In fact, as he did in most trials, Alan had emerged a victor! Alan's measuring stick for success was within. No fanfare, just being Alan and liking it. It almost made my sacrifice seem worth it. Almost.

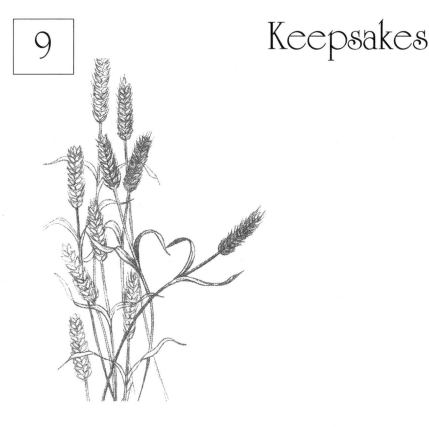

9 Keepsakes

In the hall outside the bedrooms that my siblings and I shared sat a very large antique trunk, a relic from the days my great-great-grandfather and his bride sailed from Stavanger, Norway, to the land of unlimited opportunity. Painted in tall bold letters on the side of the trunk was, *NILS HANSON BURRES, Destination: UNITED STATES OF AMERICA.*

This was a trunk that had been around. First it arrived in the New York City harbor, and after getting "processed," the trunk traveled with its new owners by train to Clayton County in northeast Iowa. There the newlyweds stopped briefly in Calmar, Iowa to visit with other Norwegians—some relatives, newly arrived themselves—to learn of this new land, its customs and its laws. When they felt ready, they moved on, settling some 60 miles away in a community of trees filled with eagles' nests, a town appropriately named Eagle Grove. The trunk held the bride and bridegroom's personal belongings, along with valuable mementos from each of their parents given to these two individuals who, after being united in marriage, set sail to begin a new life on their own in a new land. The year was 1849.

The historic old trunk had been passed down to my parents; of all the relatives who wanted it, my parents were deemed worthy of being its new guardians.

Mother made it clear that this trunk was to remain *undisturbed* at all times. We children were not sit on it, stand on it or play too near it. "Don't go near the trunk!" Mom called to us from downstairs when she overheard our routine bedtime rough-housing. Also wise to too much silence, she sometimes issued the command whether or not we sounded reckless.

Besides being a family heirloom, the trunk was functional; its contents were kept under lock and key. Only Mom had the key to this beautiful big old wooden box with the decorative and sturdy hinges and the huge metal lock. When we asked our mother what was in the trunk she said, "Just old things that you wouldn't be interested in." So for sure, we were. We were certain the trunk held treasures of great worth.

Children rarely like anything kept from them. The trunk's off-limits status only piqued our interest in getting into it. Perhaps because we were forbidden to go near the trunk, it was all the more enticing. Or perhaps we were just mischievous kids. Either way, our goal was to open that trunk.

The excuse for deliberately disobeying our mother's order came on a day we children didn't get our way. We had talked our mother into an afternoon of swimming at the pool in town and she was prepared to take us. That is, until Dad vetoed the idea because he thought we should be walking beans (pulling weeds from the beanfield) instead. We were pretty upset with her for siding with Dad; this called for retaliation. We kids huddled. A break-in plan was devised. The next day our mother had to go into town to help out at the church for a local wedding. While she was away, we would open that precious trunk and search its mysterious contents.

From bobby pins to screwdrivers to fingernail files, breaking into the trunk proved to be a challenge. And great fun. The thrill of illegally picking the lock quenched our thirst for doing that which was banned, and relieved the injustice we felt at being denied access. After nearly a half hour of trying, we succeeded! It took three children to hoist the heavy lid up and back to where it rested on steel hinges.

An initial first glance at the contents of the trunk proved Mom right. The trunk contained "just old things"—mostly keepsakes meaningful to my mother. But we felt obligated to sort through them anyway; losing out on an afternoon at the local town swimming pool with friends was quite a sacrifice. Besides, we might find real treasure underneath all this junk.

The trunk had three layers. The first layer of things were contained in a wooden bin that had three straps with tiny silver buckles to keep the items in place. We loosened the buckles and began our exploration. This top layer consisted mostly of mementos of our childhood. On the very top rested the mandatory year-by-year school shots—the ones your parents felt obligated to buy whether or not your grin in the photo made you look goofy. We looked over these photos and discussed the notion that when one of us became President (of the United States) we were going to do away with the practice of school photos because, we felt, these photos were symbolic of snobbery and revealed to classmates if you were popular. Or weren't. Not all classmates asked you to exchange photos and when they didn't, it wasn't a good feeling. That, of course, was unfair. We promised each other that whoever became President first would ban this wayward activity.

This layer also housed the snippings from each child's very first haircut, wrapped carefully in plastic bags. Given that the six of us siblings had blonde hair when we were small and blonde hair each year throughout childhood, saving dead hair seemed like an odd sort of thing for a mother to do—a perspective that, when you are raiding a forbidden trunk because you are upset with your mother, made her seem all the more like an ogre—and us more justified in our lawless actions.

Though we found the remnants of first haircuts peculiar, we also found them revealing. They were evidence of our hierarchy and confirmed the power of established pecking order. Aside from the fact that the girls' hair was braided and the boys' hair was not, the length of locks got shorter and shorter with each successive child's birth. Just as parents take too many photos of the first-born and then fewer and fewer photos of each child thereafter, so it was with the length of the hair in each bag. Judy was the oldest child. Her braid measured about nine inches in length. I was the second child; mine measured about six inches. Mark, the oldest boy, had a little bag filled with golden locks. Kevin, the second brother and child number four, had the same kind and size of bag as his older brother, but his bag held much less hair than Mark's. Tim, the youngest boy, had even less hair in his bag than Kevin. And the youngest child, Laurie, had but an obligatory swatch of hair in her bag—just enough to notice that she had grown hair at all!

Next to the locks of hair were small bags containing the first front teeth of each child. We found this keepsake even more odd than the idea of saving dead hair, and wondered why parents didn't save more important things, like hair and teeth of our favorite pets, or the dead bugs we had collected over the years. The second layer was less exciting than the first layer, with the exception of one item that held special interest at least to my sister Judy and me. Carefully wrapped in many layers of old newspaper was a large greeting-card box wherein crouched the shell of a crab. Judy forbade the smaller brothers and sister to handle this item because it was Ollie the Crabbie—a remnant of a magical day some years back when our parents had taken us for a Sunday drive and we had stopped by a small seafood roadside vendor and purchased a cooked crab to eat. It was a special day, and the shell of the crab housed the memories of a number of good feelings, especially those symbolizing our family joy and togetherness.

Next, in a tightly bundled stack bound by a thick, aged and dirty rubber band were love letters from my father to my mother and my mother to my father. Since we could only understand parts of them at that time, we dismissed any ambitious passion that the letters contained. These epistles didn't really excite our attention until we were in our teens, and by then we were either giving or getting our own love letters, so those between our parents seemed neither as torrid or risqué as we would have liked. (Though having reread these as an adult, I later changed my mind!) Completing this layer was a folded red tablecloth, the one my mother had purchased and used and then put away immediately after she and Dad shared the first meal she cooked for them in married life. [Author's note: when my mother read this story, she gave me *that* very tablecloth!]

The third layer revealed personal keepsakes from our mother's mother. Wrapped in secondhand tissue paper, now discolored by age, was the first doily my grandmother ever crocheted. A tattered piece of old tape in its corner carefully dated the beginning of its artistic life span—1912. Beneath it were two well-worn pillow cases, embroidered with small black kittens playing with a ball of string. My mother's baptismal gown was there—sewn by hand in 1881 by the family's great-great Grandma Anderson, and passed down through the generations. Alongside it was another treasure again passed down from one generation to the next, the well-used family Bible. The Bible was bestowed upon my mother on her confirmation day and would one day be placed in the hands of each of her children on their confirmation day. Next rested our mother's great-great-grandmother's hand-painted china doll. It was as tall as our biggest doll (18 inches). We studied the doll closely, noting how strange it was that a doll should look more like a beautiful lady than a beautiful baby. Our dolls looked like babies, not adults, and were made of durable rubber. This "person doll," as we called her, had a beautiful porcelain head, hands and feet, and hair that was carved into the porcelain. The body and arms and legs were filled with sawdust contained in a thin cheesecloth-like material. Attached to the sawdust arms were hands and fingers of porcelain. At the end of the doll's sawdust legs were black porcelain laced-up boots. The doll-person was dressed in a tight-fitting white bodice, a small flowered black skirt, and long white pantaloons. We thought it unlikely that the doll could withstand the rigors of our play activities.

Having explored the full contents of the chest and not finding the "crown jewels" cleverly hidden amidst all that old stuff, we discussed the possibility that all these worthless items were merely clues or a code that would lead us to the "real" treasure at some later date. From that day on, the contents of the chest remained undisturbed—with the exception of those times when my sister or I had been duly punished for a crime one or the other of us had committed but neither would fess up to. At those times when we were in mourning together, we would open the trunk and take out Ollie the Crabbie, and by recalling the fond memories surrounding the day he had come into our lives, we consoled ourselves. Remembering how wonderful our lives had been in the days of Ollie the Crabbie helped us get into the art of moaning about how awful our lives were during the time we were being punished.

In later years we asked Mom when she might share with us the items in the trunk. When you are "mature," she said.

Over the years all of us have become parents ourselves, and all of us have began our own collection of treasures. Each of us—three women and three men—possesses a trunk of some sort, though certainly not of the magnitude or scope of history as our parents'. Each of our trunks is the residence of the important memories we have created in our own families. We are accumulating keepsakes. We, too, have saved locks from our children's first year as well as babies' first teeth and first pairs of shoes. (Two siblings have had their children's first shoes bronzed, one on each side of a frame of the child's picture. Lo and behold, my daughter's first shoes are bronzed and encased as book holders!) All six siblings have kept photos and love letters from our first true loves (three of the six children married the first and only person we dated), marriage certificates, an assortment of year-by-year school photos and the like.

As we children "matured," Mom began giving us some of the items in her trunk. Now our trunks are home to new history and old history; to our children's legacy and to our own.

We adult children have talked about the commingling of the items from our mother's trunk with that of our own trunks, and speculate on the meaning of trunks. Perhaps, we think, in addition to holding contents, a trunk holds some glaring truths. The most obvious truth from our mother's trunk is that women of our mother's generation may have been the keepers of keepsakes.

We noticed that our mother's trunk held not one relic of my father's family or his childhood, yet we were quite sure that Dad must have had hair in childhood; surely some photos of him and his family were taken; there must have been family items such as Bibles and baptismal gowns that were passed from one generation to the next that were worthy of being preserved. Yet none exist.

We wondered if our foremothers' men believed preserving keepsakes to be women's work and since it was, that men need not participate in it. Or did their men consider the preserving of items such as baby's first teeth, first shoes, swatches of hair and the like, a silly but tolerable thing that *women* do? Or was storing such items considered so important that it was *left for women* to do? If this *was* women's work, were men aware of the cherished mementos and the contribution of these items in creating history and a legacy for future generations?

Such questions gave rise to the noticeable discrepancy between what seems to be true for my mother's trunk and that of her children's. For example, each of the three brothers says he is sentimental about the keepsakes stored in his trunk and can speak to the importance of the memories they represent. Each of the brothers is proud of the fact that he has participated—along with his wife—in what becomes a keepsake and why.

We also noticed that our parents safeguarded and concealed the contents of their trunk, while we children do not. What is stored in our trunk one year may be on display in our homes the next, and stored away again the year after that. We frequently hold discussions with our children about what the keepsakes are and what they represent. In some instances these items are used by our children or in some way become a part of their lives. As an example, in fourth grade my daughter was feeling "oblong and ugly." Having looked like Cinderella throughout her childhood, she wondered aloud how nature could have dealt her such a cruel blow—now she was gangly and uncoordinated, facial features elongating and filling out, not all at the same time. She complained and complained, and no reassurance on my part could appease her.

One day my daughter and I were going through the contents of the hope chest her father had given me when we were engaged to be married. We came across all the childhood pictures of me— and for me—that my mother had kept. These were of great interest to her, one more so than the others. The particular photo that caught her attention was me with an extraordinarily goofy grin on my face, oversized front teeth with the two on either side missing, looking, as she described, like the "ultimate geek." She flipped the photo over and there, in my mother's beautiful handwriting, was, "Bettie in fourth grade." My daughter rolled on the floor with laughter!

With a better understanding that a picture is worth a thousand words, I gathered up my childhood photos later that day, arranged them in a year-by-year chronology and had them put into one large frame. I hung this array of photos in the hallway outside her room. My daughter visited these photos quite often over the years. I have no doubt that they helped her accept her stages of growth.

Lately my siblings and I have been discussing how our parents see us more and more as "mature." This concerns us. Each year Mother gradually transfers more of these heirloom memories from her trunk to ours. And while we gladly take them in, we also know of their significance. Slowly letting go of one's early history is in itself a recognition of one's own letting go.

And so it is that the value of the treasures hidden in the chest have become apparent. They are treasures after all. And we realize that they are something more—keepsakes are precious symbols of a family's passage of time together on this earth. Each item is a treasure that captures the essence of a select gift of a certain time, a certain milestone—if only in one's mind. Keepsakes possess the power to capture and evoke the emotions, feelings, sights and sounds of significant events in a family's life together. Now we are certain that the treasures were always there; they just required the passage of time and perspective—our own—to see their true value. Which makes us take notice of yet another truth about keepsakes. They represent a passage of *our* time, too.

As our parents pass on these little but precious items, their stature in our hearts increases as does their value to us, precisely because they're about *time*—the times of our lives. And the time we have left to live it.

10

A Rule's a Rule!

"Coach" VanHouton was the history teacher. His only facial expression was a scowl. He practiced this face so much that the heavy lines around his mouth were not only shaped like the arches of his bushy eyebrows, but ran in the same direction. He loved coaching. He hated teaching. On the wall next to his desk hung a poster that read, "You got to jump when I say jump, sleep when I say sleep. Otherwise, you're just wasting my time." The quote was from trainer Jack Blackburn and was originally meant for the young Joe Lewis.

We didn't call him Mr. VanHouton, but rather, Coach VanHouton. He liked that. Like Jack Blackburn, VanHouton got right to the point. "Around here, a rule's a rule, and rules rule!" he declared the very first day of class. VanHouton had very few and very simple rules. Coming late to class was one of his pet peeves, and if any one student did, that student would have to stand up for the duration of the class. And VanHouton especially disliked it when students chewed gum in class—as I found out the hard way.

Carolyn Brown had taught me the art of chewing gum in class without getting caught and I had experienced a great deal of success with her technique in other classes. The Carolyn Brown Method failed in VanHouton's class.

On February 8, at 1:45, while lecturing on the Alien and Sedition Laws, VanHouton got up from his desk and, taking long deliberate strides, shuffled over to my desk. With an enormous hand parked next to my mouth, he drawled, "Miss Burres, deposit your gum right here!" He dropped his eyes in the direction of his hand. As my heart was banging against my chest cavity, I spit my wad of gum in the palm of his gigantic hand. He then issued a most unforgettable threat: "Miss Burres," he glared, "never, never, never chew gum in my class again."

The very long beautiful blonde hair that had taken me so long to grow, and that I kept meticulously groomed, hung in big curls down the middle of my back—but not when he was finished. While he continued on with the history lecture, Coach VanHouton transferred the gumwad from his palm to the back of my head, and then with both hands, picked up heavy strands of my long hair and scrunched them together. VanHouton had rubbed that piece of gum into nearly every one of the hair follicles on my four years' worth of hair.

Looking around the classroom, he said nonchalantly, "Does anyone have any questions?" Since no one knew if he meant questions about the Alien and Sedition Laws or about learning that gum was not to be chewed in his class, no one said a word.

Satisfied that there were no questions, he turned and hulked back to his messy desk.

As I was leaving the classroom that day Coach VanHouton called me up to his desk. Peering over his eyeglasses, he asked, "Do you get it?" I had no idea what he was talking about. Luckily, he didn't wait for a reply.

"You're spending far too much time in this class misdirecting your energy, Miss Burres. The cat-and-mouse game you insist on playing to see if I will catch you chewing gum on the sly takes away from your being a good student in this class. And you've been doing that for some time, haven't you?" He lowered his head and peered over the top of his bifocals, looking me in the eyes.

"Yes," I said meekly.

"I suggest you give it up," he said. "If you spent your time listening and concentrating in class, you could be a better student. Couldn't you?"

"Yes," I said quietly.

"You're bright but you're squandering your potential," VanHouton continued. "Perhaps after today you'll stop cheating yourself and instead spend your time on worthwhile things. Think you can stop spending so much time testing the rules, and just follow them?"

I could see this was going to be a long lecture. "Yes," I again said meekly.

"Following rules is about focus, Miss Burres. Focus is about self-discipline; self-discipline is necessary if you are to get good at something. Vince Lombardi once said, 'The quality of a person's life is in direct proportion to his commitment.' I suggest you stop insisting that *I* be in charge of your behavior, and take responsibility for it *yourself*. Think you can do that?"

"Yes," I said with enthusiasm. I was sure the lecture was coming to an end. I was wrong.

"The price you paid today was a big one, but I think you're worth it. There were two other students chewing gum in class that I could have picked on. I don't think my busting them would have deterred you at all. The lesson I'm trying to convey to you is not just about gum chewing. I don't mind you questioning a rule, nor is questioning authority all bad; but I suggest you pick your issues more carefully—and keep your best interest in mind when you do that. Write this down: 'A rule is about the pursuit of excellence and self-mastery.'" He repeated it three times.

"Got it?" he asked.

"Yes," I said as I scribbled across my notebook, "A rule is about the pursuit of excellence and self-mastery."

"I'd like you to take responsibility for policing yourself. Hopefully after today you will stop focusing on getting good at chewing gum on the sly, and get good at history," he said. "There is no more nobler pursuit than mastery over our own selves. Learn to exercise discipline over your own mind and train its thoughts. Focus, self-discipline, responsibility—these are common elements in almost every successful endeavor. Think about it."

"I will," I assured him, and dashed out of his room and on to my next class.

That evening as my mother cut my beautiful long hair, I was very angry at Coach VanHouton, but even more upset with myself.

"What did you learn?" Mom asked.

"That a rule is the pursuit of excellence and self-mastery," I said assuredly. "And," I added, "in VanHouton's class, a rule's a rule."

Undoubtedly knowing that my lesson had already been learned, Mom smiled and asked nothing more.

11

Rhubarb Pie

Our farm, with a sprawling 40 acres of homestead, was ideal for our large family of six children and the many pets who considered themselves one of us.

A half-acre garden grew to the east of our house; to the right of the garden grew the rhubarb patch. The garden received mixed reviews. It produced fresh vegetables, but it also needed constant attention and occasionally we children had to "serve time" in the garden—for an injustice committed or just to keep idle hands busy—hoeing and pulling weeds. With the rhubarb patch, however, all associations were positive.

The rhubarb patch never required weeding. So determined to dominate this little plot of soil, each and every spring—according to Mother Nature's time clock—the rhubarb sprouted forth, pushing aside and crowding out any weed that dared get in its way. Aesthetically, with enormous rich green leaves and tall, hearty stalks painted in various hues of pink, green and purple, the rhubarb plants were quite a regal sight.

Aside from being willful and majestic, the plants were also mysterious and enchanting. From dusk to dawn, the heavily veined leaves of the mature plants drooped themselves over the tightly coiled baby leaves as though to protect them and to allow the tiny leaves to suckle droplets of their dripping dew. But as planet Earth made its daily rotation to face the Sun, the larger leaves abandoned their caretaking roles and instead turned their long necks skyward to bask in the glorious morning light. Now exposed, the smaller leaves were seduced into awakening; slowly they unfolded their palms and drank in the rays, nourishing their fruit below.

Beauty deceived their taste! Saying that a young, tender stalk of raw rhubarb tastes significantly better than does a mature stalk, while true, isn't saying much. And we children knew first hand. "Last one to the house (or the barn, mailbox, shed, school bus, garden, you name it) has to eat an entire stalk of rhubarb!" Amongst my brothers and sisters, being a "rotten egg" for finishing last in a dare wasn't enough; having to eat a stalk of the tart, acidic rhubarb was far and away more of an incentive to join in the game and to cooperate competitively!

We children knew well the taste of rhubarb—both raw, and cooked and sweetened as a dessert.

In the spring and summer my mother performed the seasonal ritual of harvesting the young tender stalks. I often watched her gather them: long coffee-brown hair loosely tied back with a ribbon, joyously humming and singing as she went about selecting the best of the stalks from the patch, carefully laying them in the flowered apron that protected her full-skirted, flower-print dress.

The lovely vision of my mother gathering the rhubarb took second place only to the life she helped them lead once they reached our kitchen. Here Mother transformed the tart stalk into scrumptious pies and puddings and other desserts for our family. Those that weren't immediately used were placed into plastic bags and began their hibernation in the freezer, awaiting their turn for use in the late fall and winter months.

Our family loved the way Mother prepared desserts from rhubarb and looked forward to the time when they were served. Of these, our favorite was the rhubarb pie. This is not to say it was the only pie we enjoyed; goodness knows there were many—cherry, blueberry, mulberry, blackberry, strawberry, peach, apple and pecan—all made by my mother, yet none had the following of her rhubarb pie. Perhaps this was because the rhubarb pie, as Mother made it, was absolutely delicious—and because we knew and appreciated the time and toil involved, the rhubarb pie was symbolic of our mother's loving willingness to do for her family.

Often the rhubarb desserts were prepared by Mother's efforts alone; at other times she involved us fully in the process. Sometimes we made rhubarb-strawberry pudding or rhubarb-custard pudding or other variations, but making the pastry for the rhubarb pie, and filling it, was our most favorite thing to do. Always teaching, Mother showed us how to wash the long stalks and carefully cut them into $1/2$-inch cubes, enough for the 3 cups needed for a rhubarb pie (sometimes two or three pies were made at the same time). These were placed in a bowl and mixed with 1 cup of sugar, 1 teaspoon of ground cinnamon (or 2 tablespoons of chopped candied ginger), 1 tablespoon of butter, 1 egg and 1 tablespoon of cornstarch. This mixture was then set aside and we turned our attention to making the pie crust.

Meticulously, our mother taught us how to accurately measure out the cup and a half of flour, 6 tablespoons of butter, ¼ cup of water and the half teaspoon of salt needed for the pie crust. Patiently, she helped us learn how to roll out the pastry larger than the pie dish, cut away the outer strip of pastry, lay it on the dampened rim of the dish and brush it with water.

At this point the fruit mixture was packed into the pie dish, mounding it high in the middle, and the "pastry lid" was laid over the filling and trimmed to fit the unbaked pie. As a finishing touch, Mother decorated the pie crust by pinching the dough on the rim into small, even scallops, and allowed each child to use a knife to make one small slit in the pastry top to allow steam to escape during cooking.

Mother then placed the pie in the oven and set the timer. While the pie was baking, we children embarked on another exciting venture—left-over dough was rolled, pummeled, slapped, twisted, poked and shaped into designs of our own imaginations. On these we sprinkled candied sugars, raisins, nuts and chocolate chips (sometimes pieces of carrot strips and peas or small pieces of rhubarb were used for eyes or buttons or for decorations). Our "do-dads," as we called them, were then placed on a flat baking tin and put into the oven—though many were eaten raw and never reached the oven!

Brrring! Finally, the timer announced the magical moment we'd all been waiting for and we all gathered around to see what the oven had done to our pie. The fruits of our labor were about to be realized. Breathlessly we watched as Mother removed our masterpiece from the oven and placed it on the table. Seeing it in all its golden majesty and inhaling its warm, sweet aroma gave each one of us a great sense of accomplishment. For small children, the feeling of mastery and satisfaction was nothing less than what Michelangelo experienced when at last he completed his paintings on the ceiling of the Sistine Chapel. Our pie was perfect. We needed only to look at our mother's smiling face for confirmation.

Perhaps because the rhubarb pie was always present for holidays, birthdays and other special events, it became synonymous with joy and festivity. Whatever the reason, the rhubarb pie was ever-popular, and grew in stature and importance as time went by. Soon we all left home and began lives of our own. But we returned to the family nest to share our joys, our woes—and rhubarb pie. Later, when we adult children brought home spouses and children of our own, a rhubarb pie was always prepared as a homecoming and greeted us from the middle of the kitchen table as we entered the family home. And when we were ready to leave, there—accompanying hugs, wet eyes and third-time goodbyes, nestled beside a care basket of homemade breads, jams and *kringlas*[1]—sat a rhubarb pie, no doubt prepared and then hidden away for the occasion of departure.

The rhubarb pie became symbolic of Burres family unity in celebration and in comfort. It endures today—a symbol of taste, time, togetherness.

It is hard, though not impossible, to find rhubarb in all grocery stores. And it can't be found in all restaurants, but in some it will be on the menu. Maybe you will want to remedy this as I have; I've planted my own rhubarb patch. And every time I go out to pick from it, I wear my mother's flowered apron, the many-times-patched one that I begged her to give me when she said it had seen its finest hour. And I hum and sometimes sing as I prune the patch or pick from it—with the intent of making a pie

---

[1] A Norwegian pastry often served with coffee or tea. It takes the place of cake or cookies.

or giving some of the beautiful stalks to a friend, or sometimes just to call forth the lovely sight of my mother gathering the rhubarb in her apron and, with her children gathered around, rolling pie crust with her mother's mother's rolling pin.

Though I can make a mean rhubarb pie, it just doesn't quite taste like the one that my mother serves. So when I make rhubarb pie, I call her just to tell her how much I enjoyed all those rhubarb pies and the work that went with them. And how wonderful it is to be her daughter.

12 And a Child Shall Lead...

I have so many shortcomings; I can hardly believe that God entrusted you to my care. To run an organization, yes. To help others sharpen intellectual prowess, yes. But to help an innocent little being, one as precious and magnificent—and complex—as you develop sound emotional health? I am so inadequate.

You came anyway.

You knew how busy I was. There are so many things for me to do and learn in this lifetime. I am compelled to fulfill my willful curiosity about life and its mysteries. I find it such a joyous adventure; the world is so big; my work so interesting; there is so much to do and so little time.

Adapted from *How to Develop Self-Esteem in Your Child: 6 Vital Ingredients*, New York: Fawcett, 1992. © Bettie B. Youngs, Ph.D., Ed.D.

I have other excuses for not taking more time to show you the way. Are you a lesson? *My* lesson? Did you come to show me the way?

You have done both, my child.

I have been fortunate in my life to have had so many exemplary teachers, the likes of Glenn Pinkham, Ardath Bergfall, Ted Kappas, Dick Sweeney, Marie Fielder, Vic Preisser, J. Bruce Francis, Joe D. Batten—all honorable, colorful, unforgettable, wonderful people who believed in me, opened doors for me, encouraged me, mentored me. Each has deeply influenced my life in many ways. But it was you, my daughter, who has been my greatest teacher; you have touched my heart and soul unlike anything I have known. It is from you that I have learned the most intense and *extraordinary* lessons. Parenting you, Jennifer, being your mother, has offered some of the most profound insights. It has been an impassioned exercise in perfecting my own nature, and often difficult precisely because of that. It has been joyous, yet arduous; and sometimes painful.

The awesome task of parenthood has helped me focus more clearly on the meaning of my own personal journey; this has kept me from sleepwalking through life. Seeking to understand can sometimes be uncomfortable work. Parenting *you* forces me to take stock of my values and to clean house on them—sometimes refining, sometimes overhauling, sometimes being challenged to become big enough to readily practice a value I endorse but don't always follow. The desire to be a good parent causes me to examine and reconcile duplicities, to take a stance on those things for which I can be counted upon. By virtue of needing to get organized and prioritize that which gives meaning—or causes turmoil—I live more fully than I might otherwise. Loving you as I do causes me to look beyond my own needs and to care *deeply* about yours. Caring and doing are different, though, and when I am unable to meet your needs, the pain is a searing one. Pain can be a catalyst for growth. Caretaking you, dear daughter, alters my feelings of aloneness Sometimes this makes me feel burdened with a sense of responsibility; at other times I feel so lucky to be needed.

In the process of helping you climb the ladder of childhood and learn skills to surmount the challenges found each step of the way, I discover that teaching you how to pass the test of life quite often presents *me* with a learning curve, too. I've learned that I don't always have the answer key—but for certain, I wish I did.

In living with you, Jennifer, in loving you, in being a soulmate and helpmate as you learn and grow, you have taught me:

About love:
By loving you, I tapped into a reservoir of love, and find it bottomless. I didn't know I could love so much. Nor was I aware just how much this emotion would forever bond me to you, causing me to *always* be concerned about your well-being. I learn that love can be painful. I hurt when you hurt. Likewise, in those times when life rewards you and finds you worthy of its trophies, loving you as I do makes me cry in joy for your joy. I find, at times, that the line between caretaking and co-dependency is a fine one.

Joy:
As a result of my efforts, I see you prosper as a healthy, intelligent and compassionate person. Likewise, I am aware that when you fall short, its origin may be of my doing.

Happiness:

By myself with you, I've experienced the deepest level of happiness. I learn that giving really *is* more rewarding than receiving.

Empathy:

In seeking to understand you, I have had to put myself in your place and learn the meaning of unconditional caring. Sometimes my heart aches as I watch you struggle with a lesson or learn from a potent consequence. Always I have to hold myself back from intervening, because I want to rush to your side to help you, to prevent you from experiencing hurt, even though I know these lessons are yours from which to learn.

Patience:

Even with my guidance, you experience the world through your own eyes, in your own time, at your own pace. You just can't hurry some things. Time, it appears, is the essence of many a lesson. I have had to learn to be more patient than is my nature.

Endurance:

In meeting your needs, I sometimes had to care for you when I myself was sick or had other impending responsibilities. In the face of unforeseen illness and accidents, I had to make tough decisions on my own. I learned I could. I discovered an unsuspected strength within myself. Loving you as deeply as I do, I learned that I could withstand the times when your actions caused me to be saddened or feel embarrassed—and to be there for you anyway.

To listen:

I am learning to decipher not only the various tones of your voice, but to read your feelings—often disguised in subtle behaviors—and to hear what you are *really* saying rather than what I want to hear. Many times these are different. Sometimes I am wrong.

To be responsible:

Because you are so precious to me, I accept the duties and obligations of being a parent and can be depended upon to fulfill them, even when at times I might prefer to be doing something else. You can count on me.

To seek God:

The miracle of life and your birth became the catalyst for renewing and deepening my own faith. Daily challenges teach me to continually search out my heart and turn my eyes heavenward. Praying for the redemption of my soul, *and yours*, is priority over asking for abundance.

Your needs:

By listening and observing, I am discovering what you need from me and learning that sometimes these are different from my expectations. Daily I learn how different we are. And how alike.

The *fragility* of human life:

Though this feeling began with my pregnancy, as soon as you were born I knew your life was mine to protect, and that I was committed to it at all costs. As I began to understand and value the fragility of human life, I began to take better care of my own health. Protecting your life is a compelling duty. I am often fearful. Such feelings pave the way to care about others whose lives are in jeopardy anywhere in the world—from evil, oppression, hurt, starvation or war.

Purpose:

The value of your life has given importance to "being our brother's keeper." This affirms my work and adds a crucial dimension of meaning to it. It sustains me. I teach and write what I am learning, not always what I practice. There is much "after the fact" learning. I am learning to let go and let God.

To live consciously:

Because I am being constantly observed by you, I must be aware of what I say, as well as what my actions convey. Setting a good example is an ever-present challenge. Sometimes this makes me feel caged and I must confront my selfishness; other times I am grateful for caring enough to grow. Confronting my own values up close is sometimes rewarding and at others times a bit unsettling.

Empathy for other parents:

I believe parenthood is a universal language connecting mothers and fathers everywhere. Once I sympathized with the parents of sick, crying, dying, injured or missing children; now I feel with them. Parenthood has made me realize that other parents have the same joys and sorrows as do I. Sharing in this sister/brother/parenthood is very bonding. I feel closer—as though I "know" something about those who are parents.

To grow, to evolve:
I know that I am becoming a better, wiser and more loving person than I might otherwise have been. And of course, I also learn what I am not but wish I were.

To set priorities:
After I accepted that my days were not going to suddenly get longer simply to accommodate my expanded responsibilities, I resigned myself to the fact that my desire for perfection just had to go. I've learned that while some things must be done, other things are a matter of choice—even people. Those who stimulate and motivate, inspire or encourage me are crucial to my wellness; people who drain me and are not supportive, are jaded or negative or insist on seeing the cup half-empty, must find friendship elsewhere.

To be efficient and effective:
Once set-backs made me disappointed, confrontations sped up my heart rate. Energy that used to be spent on tension and anxiety is now channeled into getting things done efficiently and effectively. There is a difference between doing things right and doing the right things. Other people appreciate it, too. They don't want people around who are stressed out—they want to be around those who are leading their lives effectively, and with efficiency and style. When you're in the position of having other people depend on you—at home or at work—thinking with clarity and being consistent and assertive is essential.

To lead:

Parenting is about leadership. When your actions are always being observed and scrutinized, you learn quickly from your mistakes and readily feel your accomplishments. I learned to leverage my time wisely. Self-discipline leads to accomplishments and productivity; these have contributed to and generated a positive sense of self-regard.

That parenting is forever:

When you were an infant I looked forward to a time when you would be able to play independently, and when you could, you still looked around to see if I was there. When you were in grade school, your intellect was insatiable and the need for instilling rules and guidelines to help you operate safely in the outer world was a must. Your abundant activities in junior high school required multiple bandages and a daily carpool; your quest and need to understand your feelings sometimes made me feel like a clinical psychologist with you as my entire caseload.

Now that you are a young adult, you need to know your place in the world and to understand that the dynamics of relationships on an experiential basis occupy a good portion of your waking hours. Just as I worried when you were little that you might stick a finger in a light socket or be treated badly by another child, I worry now that you might leave a stove burner on (or an iron or hot rollers), or that you or another driver will exercise poor judgment while in a two-ton car. I want to protect you from being emotionally devastated in relationships, even though you must learn such lessons first hand.

Perhaps my concerns will go on for some time. Just yesterday my mother called and lovingly expressed her concerns for my safety on my upcoming trip abroad, though I have made the same journey nearly 20 times over the past 25 years.

To forgive my parents:

The constancy of parenting, the work, the responsibility, the ever-present concern of wondering if I am bringing out the best in you—helping you find and develop your abilities, talents and goodness—is a lingering one. I often struggle with the juggle of being true to my own needs, yet being there for you. This duplicity is insightful and helps me to forgive my parents for the ways they didn't know me but I expected them to, and for the experiences they didn't provide me, but I wished they had.

Parenthood has taught me that parenting is by design, an exercise in completing one's own unfinished business of childhood. I've come to realize that children are little creatures who come to us with their own spiritual history, and as such, every child-and-parent relationship is unique. While parents can devise a master plan, each child comes with his or her own needs for caretaking, individual in the purpose to be lived out in an earthly lifetime. Understanding this helps me judge less, and honor more, the parental actions of my parents.

To honor my parents:

It has been a serious undertaking to show you that I both love you and respect you, that I accept you for who you are—especially during those times when I disapprove of your actions. Mother was right; little children step on your feet, big children step on your heart. It has taken many moons to help you prepare to live interdependently in the world; it may take many more. It's been a daily exercise of setting appropriate expectations and consistently encouraging and motivating you in living purposefully; sometimes this is tedious and thankless work. This causes me to value the efforts of my parents, and to honor not only their parenting actions, but the efforts of their intentions as well.

Daughter of mine, teacher of mine. Always you are on my mind. I am the possessor of a heart that loves you so much! When can I quit being a mother, a student? When can I stop caring *so much*?

Thank you, Jennifer, for choosing me to help you find your way in this world. I am so genuinely sorry for all the ways I have let you down, and for not always praying enough for insight and guidance. Though sometimes I thought I knew what to do or could figure it out, in some ways I didn't have a clue; sometimes it wasn't until afterwards that I learned if what I did (or didn't do) was, or wasn't, good for you.

Interestingly, I tried to be the parent to you that, while I was growing up, I wanted my parents to be for me. Ironically, just as my parents weren't always the parents I wanted them to be, you, too, have found that I haven't always done what you wanted or been what you needed. Alas, *the same snow that covers the ski slopes makes the roads to them impassable.*

Thank you for choosing me anyway, for having the courage to take a chance on me. Though it was I who was your parent, it was you who were my teacher. You are the greatest lesson—and teacher—of all.

Thank you Mom and Dad, for all your day-after-day parenting, year after year. Thank you for giving me the experience of two loving parents under the same roof throughout childhood. I had no idea how difficult this is to pull off. Thank you for bandaging up all my physical wounds and for comforting me in the emotional ones, and for not being the cause of any of them.

Thank you for the depth and breadth and richness of the friendship we share. Thank you for allowing me to be, with you, all things—to stumble, to be powerful; to come to you for advice, to be needed by you when you need advice. Thank you for your example of authenticity, honesty, simplicity, self-discipline, courage and quality, and for teaching me the need to live a principle-centered life. These core values, when applied, withstand the many tests in my life.

Your lives are of great worth to me. You have instilled both the need and the framework for the attainment of nourishing values. As a result, my life is full of meaning, full of fun, full of joy, full of love. It is purposeful. Now older and wiser, I know the importance of your shortcomings as well as your strengths; both have added to my curiosity, determination and ambition for living my life as I have. I now see more clearly why it was the both of you I needed as my parents. Thank you for loving me because you knew me so well; thank you for loving me in spite of knowing me so well. Eternally, I will always be thankful that I have been loved so much. Always your spirit will travel with me as I complete my own earthly journey, and when it's time for you to move on to God's next assignment, be reassured that I will continue to draw strength from the simple, powerful relationship we share.

Thank you, God, for my parents and for my Jennifer. My life has been so enriched by these earthly angels. Jennifer is an adult now and exerting her will upon the world. She is facing a great number of value-laden decisions, at a time when she must make more independent decisions than interdependent ones. I stand at a distance and watch, sometimes proudly and other times with hopeful eyes, as she puts into practice her interpretation of what I have imparted. As she goes about asserting her will upon the world and touching lives, I feel like a distressed yet hopeful contestant at a pageant awaiting that moment of decision. Please, God, allow her to win at life.

Being a parent has been the most difficult assignment I have ever been given, God. I have not always done so well; like so many parents, I wish I could do it over, knowing what I know now. But if you will allow me more time within this relationship with this child I love so much, if you will continue to have faith in me for her *continued* care, I promise to do better. Please, God, care for her when I cannot. When I do not.

I will continue to worry and fret over her as my parents still do with me. Wherever she shall travel or rest her head, I can think of no greater honor than to be her "Mom." Though she has grown into an independent young woman, I know that I play a key role in her wellness. We seem to be inextricably tied. Please, God, give her a sense of interdependence.

I want to love her into eternity. In the meantime, I look forward to Jennifer being a parent herself, and to a time when it's her turn to learn firsthand, through her own children, those lessons we parents learn in parenthood. I most definitely look forward to knowing her children and can think of no greater privilege than bestowing upon them all the goodness a grandmother can. Please, God, give my Jennie moral friends, true happiness, insight and the gift of love.

Humbly, I ask all this of you, God, for I have so many shortcomings, and she is so precious and worthy. Above all, God, *thank you* for my Jennifer—and for such a wonderous and worthy assignment.

13

Queen of Extreme

When writer Jenny Joseph wrote, "When I am old I shall wear purple with a red hat which doesn't go . . . spend on summer gloves and satin sandals . . . go out in my slippers in the rain . . . and pick flowers in other people's gardens . . . maybe I'll start now . . . ," she could have been inspired by Patti.

Patti never hesitated to be precocious, flagrant or excessive. She didn't worry about *doing* what she wanted, or about *being* different from the rest of us. Quite simply, Patti was more colorful and had more pizzazz than the rest of her ninth-grade classmates. And she did everything with style!

Patti was also considered the most beautiful girl in the school. Consequently, we always voted her to be a cheerleader, to be on the student council or the latest queen of whatever—any excuse to put her in front of us so we could look at her without appearing obvious. Whatever the event, we willingly allowed her all categories—win, place or show.

If this fabulous creature lacked for anything, she more than made up for it in the way she prepared and presented herself to the world: delightfully extreme, outrageously playful, sophisticated camp. She was a very high-class floozy. Patti shaved off her God-given eyebrows and drew on new ones where *she* preferred to have them. She painted her lips in many shades of pink, and in many shades of red. She wore batwing eyeliner before it was fashionable and taught us that eyelashes didn't have to be merely brown or black, they could be in shades of blue; that nails could be more than long and lacquered, they could be long and plastic. She wore nylons before anyone else did—Tuesday, the third week of seventh grade, to be exact. Without one bit of shame she wore *very* padded bras before any of the other girls did and very tight sweaters to show them off. Her short tight skirts were pinched in the middle by an oversized belt that looked like it was squeezing her in two. To this she would add high heels (when the rest of us were trying to convince our parents to buy us a second pair of shoes, anything other than Van canvas shoes). And when bouffant hairdos were in, Patti back-combed her hair bigger than anyone else dared. To complete her costumes she wore lady-killer, bad-boy senior Dwight Craigton's class ring around her neck on an angora string. And when she wore his enormous ring on her finger, she wrapped in a wad of angora bigger than her knuckle and the ring combined.

Patti was quite a production: the queen of extreme, our own Dolly Parton. She was great!

We, her classmates, seemed to understand, even value, Patti's sense of individuality, and accepted that the drummer she marched to was different from our own. Perhaps it was her beauty and her grace that made it not only acceptable for us to associate with one so wild and free, but to vote her into leadership positions in school activities so that we could bask in her presence and, vicariously, be her.

So here's to the Patti in all of us! May we first of all discover it, and then allow ourselves to buy satin sandals, to pick more wildflowers, walk in the rain in our slippers, and wear purple more often. And not wait too long before we do.

14

Art the Banker

They were men of like character and values, men who found possibility and goodness in everything; and they were equally playful. Each caught fish bigger than the other; each had stalked the biggest Montana moose! They boasted and bragged to each other about their children's achievements and patiently listened with interest to redundant stories about each other's experiences in the war. Each was reverent and respectfully shy in the presence of the other's wife.

My dad was a young man starting out on a rented farm near Vincent, Iowa. He didn't have a penny to his name, but he had a big dream and an even bigger plan for making it happen. Among his few assets were a strikingly beautiful young wife, three healthy children and one on the way. He had started out with

outdated machinery abandoned by successful neighboring farmers; other necessary equipment was borrowed in exchange for his
toil. Over the years he'd pieced together what was needed to
"farm the farm."

I remember these as wonderful years for our family. Striving,
pulling together from sunup to sundown in unison. My mother
and dad were happy and optimistic. It was during that time that
he made an enormous decision for a man weighted under so
much responsibility. He decided he wanted a larger scale operation. Dad was a livestock and crop farmer—one who needed
financial backing for all of it. He had also established a reputation
as a family man, a good farmer, a decent man, ethical, honorable,
a man of good character and integrity, a man of his word—with
a mind for business. These traits were to become his collateral.

Art Swasand, the banker at the Farmer's Savings Bank in
Vincent, was an honorable man who believed in honorable men.
He did business the old-fashioned way himself; a client's charac-
ter was an important part of the deal.

The new John Deere, mortgaged and otherwise owned by the
Vincent bank, was such a major acquisition that the day Dad
brought the tractor home, Art the Banker drove over to inspect it.
He brought with him a five-pound box of Brach's chocolates "for
the Missus" with eight gold-foil wrapped candies in the top layer,
and eight gold-foil wrapped candies in the second layer. I know
because I counted them again and again over the next few weeks,
sometimes unwrapping them to see if the candy inside was still
there, and sometimes taking an itsy-bitsy bite to ensure that it
hadn't spoiled.

Art the Banker practiced customer service the old-fashioned
way, too—get involved, go the extra mile, do whatever it takes to

develop and maintain a successful working relationship and work to make the joint venture succeed. When the tractor broke down in the field one day, Art the Banker drove out and visited Dad right there in the field—white starched shirt, gray suit and all. Once he understood what was needed to get the tractor up and running again, Art financed the parts right there on the spot.

That tractor and that five-pound box of chocolates were the start of a powerful lifetime relationship. Art the Banker became one of Dad's many admirers, and I'm sure Dad felt the same about Art. Over the years, these two men financed and paid off machinery, created financial security, purchased land (and many more expensive machines) and raised their families. Without fanfare, they became prosperous men doing what they each loved best, with integrity—the old-fashioned kind.

When Art died many years later, our entire family attended the funeral. Dad wiped away tears throughout the service.

"Mom says Art's in heaven with God, Dad," I said trying to console him. "She says we should be happy. Don't you think he's in heaven?" I wondered why that possibility didn't make Dad happy instead of sad.

"Of course he's in heaven," my dad countered. "God can't afford not to have him in heaven, but he'll be very much missed here on earth. I miss his friendship already."

Dad was teary-eyed for many days.

Some years later I asked Dad if he ever thought of Art. "Oh, of course I do," he said. "To this day, every time I go to the bank I expect him to greet me." Dad said this with a wide smile on his face. "But, you know," he continued, "he's not so far away. He was with me in spirit when I bought that $123,000 combine this spring. Boy, if he could see this operation we're running now! Well, for all I know, he's still engineering it!"

Caught up in the memories, Dad continued, "Sure I think of him. When Art died I had to say goodbye to a truly great man. He gave me my first start. I was just a young guy starting out. I had no resources. My parents had lost our family farm when I was a kid and it was a pretty rough road for the family. The children were separated, as they had to work for other families in exchange for room and board. I vowed that one day I would buy the family farm back, but of course, that really wasn't possible. So then I became intent on owning land of my own and keeping my family together, and building a future for them. Art was there at a time when I needed someone to take a chance on me. Goodness knows I was a risk for him. He believed in me when he didn't need to, and he supported me through thick and thin. In more ways than one he was a father, a brother, a confidant, a friend. He was my ideal of a man. There isn't one thing I wouldn't have done for him; there certainly isn't anything he didn't do for me." Dad's voice trailed off and I could see that he was still remembering.

Then looking up toward the sky he said, "I still miss you, Art. Thanks for caring about me, and for giving me a start so that I could care for my family. Thanks for your example and brotherhood, and for helping make my dream possible."

His eyes watered over and he added, "Don't forget my offer. If there's anything you forgot to do down here, Art, just let me know and I'll get it done for you. Nothing's too big to ask of me. Nothing. Nothing at all." With a giant tanned and weathered hand, Dad wiped away the tear making its way down his cheek.

A vision crossed my mind of Art in heaven, sitting on a bench, saving Dad a seat up there next to him.

Watching the trusting bond between Art and my father throughout those years was for me an example of brotherly love in action. Perhaps we need more men like them. And we need to write of them more often.

I was saddened by my father's sadness at having loved and lost a friend so dear—and alarmed by the thought that followed. One day I would have to say goodbye to this magnificent and honorable man, my dad. Luckily, there was an instantaneous consolation: just as Art's spirit was ever present for my father, my dad's spirit would be ever present for me, too.

And surely God had need of my dad in heaven.

15

My Guardian Angel

Now I lay me down to sleep,
I pray thee Lord, my soul to keep.
If I should die before I wake,
I pray thee Lord, my soul to take.
If I should live for other days,
I pray thee Lord, to guide my way.
Bless Mom and Dad,
Judy and Mark and Kevin and Tim, and . . .
Grandma and Grandpa . . . and,
and everyone I love. . . . Amen.

Prayers were said at the foot of the bed. Every night. On our knees. Hands folded. Head bowed. Eyes closed.

"Close your eyes," Mom reminded me.

No matter how hard I tried to keep my eyes closed, I couldn't. "Mommy," I whispered, "she's watching me again."

"Of course she is," Mother replied matter-of-factly. "Now close your eyes."

I squeezed my eyes shut as hard as I could.

"Mom, even when I close my eyes I can feel her watching me." As much as I tried, I could not remove her image from my mind. Towering. Authoritative. Mystical. Majestic. Divine. Protective. Eerie.

She lived in the picture hanging over the head of my bed, a rather large angelic female creature, hovering over a sweet and innocent-looking little girl tucked in her bed.

When I kneeled to pray, I could sometimes feel the angel lift her eyes from the beautiful sleeping child in the picture and look in my direction. Other times, like now, I felt as if she had stepped out of the picture and stood next to me, her long gracious arms draped around my shoulders in a very gentle caress. Whether she stayed in the picture or stood beside me, always she fanned a gentle and warm cloud of air over me.

She was a soothing and protecting presence.

"She's putting air on me again," I informed my mother. Mom ignored me.

I tried again. "Why is she doing that, Mommy?"

"She's just looking after you," was Mom's reply. "It's her job. It's the work of guardian angels to look after little girls and keep them safe."

Safe from what, I didn't know. After all, Jesus loved me and that was guaranteed. My mother and father and my Sunday school teachers told me so. God loved unconditionally and, luckily, for always. Nothing I could ever do could mess that up.

Besides, I didn't exactly know why the guardian angel was needed. I couldn't imagine anything getting through the mighty presence of my protective parents. I wondered why guardian angels didn't take care of little boys, too. Who would look after my brothers? And did this mean that I would have to share her with my sister Judy? I hoped not because my sister was mischievous, and if the angel watched over her, too, there would be precious little time left for her to watch over me. Who watched over the little girl in the picture when the angel was with me? Do angels watch over pets, too . . . ?

"Concentrate on your prayers," Mother said.

"Can angels read my mind, too?" I said, thinking that my mother had read my mind.

"Angels know when you want them to be with you and when you don't," she replied.

"Does the angel look after me all the time? In the daytime, too?" I wanted to know.

"Yes. Always."

"Even when I am at school?" I inquired.

"Yes," Mom reassured me. "Guardian angels are always with you. Just ask for your guardian angel in your prayers or in your thoughts and she'll be there to help you."

It was an interesting idea. But for nearly 30 years I was too young and too bold and too confident and knew too much about everything to have need of her help. Until 4:00 A.M., November 7, 1990.

Is it possible for emotional pain to cause one's heart to bleed? I felt like mine was slowly dripping. The grief and despair I felt was intense and overwhelming, and I worried that I would get sick from such constantly stressful emotions.

In previous times of trial and heartache I had found comfort in Margaret Rose Powers' "Footprints." In it, a man, in reviewing the journey of his life, notices two sets of footprints in the sand, one belonging to him and the other to the Lord. He is surprised to find that many times along the path of his life there was only one set of footprints and, most especially, this happened at the very lowest and saddest times in his life. He wonders how this could be, since he had asked the Lord to always be with him. Perplexed, he asks the Lord why, during the most troublesome times in his life, at those times when he needed God most, God left him. God answers him, saying, "My precious child, I love you and would never leave you. During your times of trial and suffering, when you see only one set of footprints, it was then that I carried you."[1]

I read and reread this piece now, visualizing a beautiful and soothing vision of God carrying me through this time of pain. It offered only minor comfort. I pleaded with God. "I understand that you've been carrying me a lot recently; I look through my sand and all I see are your footsteps, so I know you have the whole load. But I feel so fragile, so bruised right now, and not at all like I can handle the challenge that lies before me. I need so much looking after, God. I've been so big and strong for so many for so long, and all I want now is to be soothed and relieved of this burden I'm carrying. I need more support and guidance than I thought." Chuckling, I added, "Do you have any angels that are willing to take me on? And do overtime?" Then, thinking that God might not take me seriously if I got comical, I changed my appeal to a more somber approach. "I'm making a mess of this alone, and really need some guidance."

---

[1] Margaret Rose Powers. "Footprints," *Guideposts*, July 1992: 34-39.

Obviously God had been waiting for me to ask, for just as I had been taught "Ask and ye shall receive," "Knock and it shall be opened unto you," instantaneously I felt a response. A divine aura of omnipotent wisdom was beside me and I felt the same sensation of being soothed and comforted—the same effects I felt as a child when I had innocently allowed the angel into my life as my guardian.

"I will watch over you," said a honey-smooth voice that felt to my ear more like a warm liquid than a sound. There appeared in my mind's eye the vision of the very angel who had hung over my bed for all the years when I was a little girl. I considered the possibility that I was hallucinating. Or perhaps the stress really had been more than I could handle.

I wondered which of those two could explain the vision of the angel, but the need to question didn't last but a moment. I didn't see the sense in being analytical; to fully experience this all-encompassing sense of peace, calm and equilibrium proved far more fruitful. To be present in the moment was compelling—my entire being was enveloped in understanding. I felt as vulnerable as I had been as a little girl kneeling beside my bed in prayer; dismantled, but not exposed; astonished, but not frightened.

I leaned into this feeling. It was in *that* moment that the burdens and pains of my heart lifted, and warm and nourishing feelings of peace replaced it.

I felt for a moment as if I may have died, and this was my escort to my next destination. Those feelings disappeared quickly, replaced by an inner knowing to everything I had questioned.

There came to me the realization that I had been spending too much time coping with an unworthy relationship, and that trying to make it work was not an appropriate use of my time and energy. There was immediate insight that the emotional pain I was feeling was a wakeup call to get back on track to seeking my own salvation, and not that of the relationship. It occurred to me that I had strayed from that which brings me joy and satisfaction and provides me with a deep sense of meaning and contentment. It also occurred to me that it was time to return to those things I had loved so much in life—such as focused time with my precious daughter, time for supportive friends and family members, the work I had chosen and that meant so much to me.

There was also an immediate understanding that the pain and heartache I was experiencing was not to punish or to hurt me, but to teach, give me experience and create an opportunity for my own growth. With this realization, many of my past experiences, even those I thought were negative, took on new meaning. No real mistakes had been made in my life. Each experience was a tool for me to learn from and was an invitation to grow; it was my chance to mature spiritually and emotionally. Even unhappy experiences allowed me to obtain greater understanding about myself, until I learned to avoid those experiences and choose, instead, more loving and enriching ones.

Other truths were unveiled to me. I realized that there were times throughout my life when my guardian angel had played a part, and in fact, that many of my experiences had been orchestrated by guardian angels. I knew there was much of my life yet to live, and within it, some experiences would be difficult, others would be joy-filled; all were calculated to bring me to highest levels of insight.

I was guided to accept that there would be many more times in my life when I would need guardian angels to assist me in fulfilling my life's purpose, mission and destiny. Once again, just as I had when I was a little girl, I implicitly trusted that my guardian angels would remain with me through my joys and my trials. In that moment, I knew that my guardian angel would always be with me to comfort and to guide, to protect and to direct. And that the responsibility of asking for this was mine.

From that moment on, I saw myself growing in my willingness to experience my unfolding, and to value who I am and who I am becoming as I evolve in my spiritual maturity. I still see myself growing in my ability to listen to and be responsive to my needs and to the needs of others. It is with conviction that I vow no longer to squander or suppress the loveliness of my own soul—even at the risk of being unpopular to loved ones, or to those whom I do not know.

I experienced a new and joyous beginning.

The next day I awoke with mixed feelings. Had I dreamed all this? I went to the kitchen for my usual morning cup of Calle tea. Wanting to sit for a moment and review the astonishing events and thoughts from the previous evening, I took my tea and headed for the outdoor patio, but stopped briefly, taking down the first book that my hand touched from the nearby bookshelf.

I casually opened the book and began reading the page in front of me. To my amazement, here in words were many of the feelings and ideas the angel had shared with me the previous night.

As I lay sleeping an angel came to me,
Saying take my hand, walk with me,
I will guide you through the storm.
Take my hand, walk with me,
And know I will always be with thee.

My angel said to me

Continue through the storm, dear one,
That you may know it all.
Continue through the storm, dear one,
That you may guide them all . . . .

Take my hand, dear one, and always walk with me.[2]

This piece found meaning in my heart; I found the words uplifting, their coincidence an omen that I must be respectful and open to the soft whispers of inspiration.

Now ready to start my day, I went to my office, opened my Daytimer and looked at the day's schedule. At the top of the page was the saying for the day:

Look for miracles in your midst. And thank God for the blessing you receive.

---

[2] Reprinted with permission, Phyllis Price, 1991, *Angels*. Virginia Beach, Virginia. A.R.E. Press, 1993.

16

Ollie the Crabbie

"You are my sunshine, my only sunshine! You make me happy when skies are gray. You'll never know, dear, . . ."

We were two little girls in the back of a brand new 1952 royal blue Ford pickup truck with our parents, then two young lovers, in the front seat. Radio blaring, my father, a young man just back from two terms of active duty in a long and brutal war now proclaimed over, was singing at the top of his lungs "You'll never know, dear, how much I love you. Please don't take my sunshine away."

For Dad, a new and different and good life was beginning. He was a happy and free man the day he unpacked his duffel bag for the last time. Finally home from World War II—in a time when the United States revered and made heroes of its protectors—Dad was about to embark on a new life: developing housing in Richland, Washington, and heading up his family.

The woman of his heart, his wife, was now more than a passionate love letter two months delayed in getting to him after traveling from the APO in San Francisco to Japan. This young and optimistic woman was now his daily companion and helpmate, not just a listener of his woes and hopes and aspirations, but a real part of the dream machine. Together they were giving birth to the life they had promised each other—with all the fervor and commitment they could muster. They had conceived more than just goals for their future: now photos displayed two little girls, laughing, clutching and clinging to their adoring parents. He felt unstoppable.

Dad loved this family just about as much as he *needed* it. Though he had managed to get out of the war without wounds, that was not true of his own early years. To be loved and to be needed by this family would be fundamental and necessary in removing the pains of his own shattered childhood; to secure his family's safekeeping would be instrumental in stitching up the enormous gashes suffered when his parents lost all their material possessions, their home included. It was crucial in removing the anguish he still felt from the time his brothers and sisters were doled out to anyone who would take them, exchanging labor for room and board. This young family was key to Dad's happiness and contentment. With this family came meaning, reason, purpose. There was plenty to live for!

Next to him was his wife, my mother. Her long, coffee-brown hair was tied back with a red ribbon that matched her red sundress lined with two rows of white rickrack. Hair, ribbon and dress blew from the wind whooshing in through the open car windows.

Mother needed this family, too, and knew of its importance to her wellness. She had lost her own beloved father when she was ten, and as child number five among nine, she needed to bond, needed connection.

For her, wanting and needing this man, now her husband, were priorities of the same urgency. It wasn't that he was a link to her future; he was her future. She needed his strength and needed his tenderness. It allowed her to act on her own enormous power. How often her gaze was transfixed on him, a man whose physical and emotional presence was as powerful as it was breathtaking. How often I had seen her look at him with tenderness and love. He knew when she looked at him; his handsome face would break into an easy and alluring smile, his velvet voice and dancing eyes would tell her of his friendship, and of his leadership, too. My father was her knight every day. That she was totally loved by this man was undeniable. Together they had created this family. Fate had planned it, she would will it to be lasting.

"You are my sunshine, my only sunshine," Dad sang in a loud, off-key, happy voice to her. Distinctly, I remember her joyous laugh.

It was one of those incredibly perfect moments when everything is right and nothing else matters—Mom was embraced by the omnipotent aura of being totally and completely cherished by the man she adored, anchored by children both wanted.

My sister and I could feel it.

Wearing matching flowered dresses made by our mother, our long curly hair uncut from the day we were born, my sister and I sat on a big quilt in the back of the truck, hair and dresses blowing in the wind. We were totally and completely enraptured by this moment of unconditional joy. We had everything: sunshine in our hair, smiles on our faces, joyous parents—out for a Sunday drive.

We were driving along the ocean in Vancouver, Washington, when my parents stopped by a roadside seafood vendor and purchased a cooked Dungeness crab to eat. Over the next stretch of road my mother would slowly and carefully dismantle this beautiful orange-red crustacean and allocate carefully picked portions to each member of her family. Slowly and ever so carefully she broke apart the crab, hand-feeding succulent pieces first to Dad, and then to her little daughters sitting in the back. "Here, girls!" she'd say lovingly. Like a mother bird feeding her young, she fed us small bites of salty and delicious tender crabmeat. The crab was picked clean from its home.

Time was suspended and the day held perfect in all ways. The taste of that moist, flavorful crabmeat was to be imprinted in all of our memories, recorded forever.

Always when I'm on the waterfront in a city I go searching for a place that serves crab, hoping to replicate the spectacular taste of the crab we had that day. And though I have ordered crab in some of the finest restaurants the world over (including a Vancouver restaurant I visited during a recent ski trip in Whistler, B.C.), and from some great back-alley eating places, too, I have never been able to duplicate the taste of the crab from that sunny balmy day in Vancouver.

Someone once said that a memory is a second chance to experience happiness once enjoyed firsthand. But what makes one impression more lasting than another? Certainly the birth of one's own baby creates an indelible imprint and evokes powerful emotions throughout one's lifetime. But a crab consumed along an ocean drive? What was the magic of this crab?

A couple of years ago on a trip to the Midwest to visit my family, I asked my sister Judy about the origin of a beautiful old heirloom teacup that sat on the top shelf of her china closet. "Oh," she said excitedly, and got up and walked to the china closet to take down the lovely cup, "this old relic is from Great Auntie Hilda's house. Garry and the kids and I have dropped this precious teacup more than once, as you can see. It's been glued a thousand times so by now it's worthless—but not its contents!"

In that instant, her demeanor transformed from her serious "mom" and "older sister" presence into a girlish, light-hearted and mischievous presence. "Look!" she said gleefully. Unable to contain her joy as she walked toward me, she tipped the cup at an angle for me to see as she approached. "Do you know who it is?" she asked, laughing merrily.

"I have no clue," I replied, baffled as to what it was.

Joyously she said, "It's the remains of Ollie!"

"Ollie?" I inquired.

"Sure, you remember Ollie," she said. "Remember that day in the back of the truck in Vancouver and how we playfully argued what we would call the crab Mom and Dad bought for us all to eat?"

I looked into the cup again and sure enough, these were tattered and fragile remains of a crab shell. I couldn't believe it.

"You've got to be kidding," I said. "This is really the shell from *that* day?"

"No doubt about it," my sister said, laughing. "Remember how we used to get into the old treasure trunk outside our bedroom—illegally of course—and take this crab out of the storage box and stroke his shell?"

Remembering that she had called him "Ollie," I corrected her. "You mean Crabbie," I said. "We nicknamed him Crabbie."

"Oh, no, we didn't," she countered good-naturedly. "You wanted to call him Crabbie, but I said he should be called Ollie. We put it to a vote. We settled on Ollie."

Experience told me that if Judy had put it to a vote, the outcome had already been decided, that the rest of the voters were merely being advised on what had been her choice. I was searching for something appropriate to say to this sister of mine who thinks she is an authority on just about everything. Wanting to preserve the warmth of the moment, I said nothing.

"Okay, I'll concede," she said, laughing again, and in the voice she owned when she was a little girl, added, "From here on out we'll call him Ollie the Crabbie. Deal?"

"Deal!" I said happily. It was a frivolous victory, given meaning only in that it was unlike Judy to compromise on anything! But she, too, was not about to let anything come between the joy of the memory of that day.

"When did you get him?" I asked.

"About three years ago when Mom was going to toss it because he was disintegrating so badly. There's practically nothing left of this shell. But this crab has held such special meaning for me all these years, so I asked Mom if I could have it. This guy Ollie, ah, Ollie the Crabbie, must have been pretty special for Mom, too, because she's kept it for some 35 years! Can you imagine? So here he is. I don't know how much longer he'll be around, but here's what's left of him!"

"Judy," I asked, "What does the crab shell represent to you? Why has it retained meaning for you all these years?"

"Oh," she said nostalgically, "It means a great deal. First of all, it brings back images of Mom and Dad in their new Ford pickup truck, so happy together, and how good that made us feel, the real sense of family togetherness. Sometimes my life gets so busy, but I wonder if I'm spending my time doing those things that matter most. When I spot the cup in the china closet, I stop and reconnect with my children. Ollie reminds me to focus on making memories of joy and love and togetherness for my family. So Ollie the Crabbie is a reminder to be a more loving spouse and parent."

"It's really that powerful?" I asked.

"Sure is," she said. "Just the other day I was babysitting my five-year-old grandson, Stephen, for my daughter, Lynda. Some months back I had shown little Stephen Ollie's remains, and on this day he wanted to see them again. I had a lot to do that day and was thinking that my grandson would be tagging along with me as I completed my errands, but after taking Ollie down and showing him once again to Stephen, I decided my 'to-do' list could wait. Instead, my grandson and I walked down to the old creek bed and caught some crayfish. It was a thrilling day for Stephen, and a really special day for the two of us. Ollie the Crabbie is still working magic, still *creating* memories."

For nearly an hour we recounted, detail by detail, the events of that joyous day in our childhoods. Some 40 years later, Ollie the Crabbie had all but deteriorated, but like a song played at a pivotal point in time that triggers a certain memory every time you hear it, the crab's shell still housed a memory symbolic of family joy in abundance. His shell was a reminder to revisit that memory again and again.

All this meaning from a simple little crab purchased on a beach by two young parents living on a shoestring, but whose love and joy were so complete that it was passed on to their children, creating the power of joy in their lives as well. A joy that is still living on.

Though his shell may not make it much longer, Ollie the Crabbie may just live forever.

17 | Sonny and Karla

"Let mourning stop when one's grief is fully expressed."
— Confucius

Tremors of spasms from weeping so deeply invaded every back muscle in the room. Shoulders rose as chests rapidly sucked in short spurts of air, but slumped as they exhaled long anguish-laden sighs. The sounds of grieving could be heard from every pew. Bewildered disbelief filled every molecule in the air. Few heads were upright; some heads rested on the shoulders of family members or friends nearby; some of the heads were bowed, many to the point of resting on their owners' chests. Faces were caressed by tissue- and handkerchief-carrying hands, busy soaking up the tears that poured from all eyes in the room.

It was the first funeral I ever attended, and it was an especially sorrow-filled experience. People in this room were saddened beyond description; bereaved family members, friends and classmates, all tormented with pangs of distress. My feelings vacillated in the various states of shock.

Two classmates, young lovers, both seniors, died together, asphyxiated by exhaust fumes from the very car in which they had pulled over to talk of their love and plans for their futures. The last day of their future had arrived.

Fumes that had funneled out of the car caught a ride on the evening's breeze and were sucked back into the car through the opening between the inner and outer panels of the fender. It was foggy and late at night. It was a fateful night.

Carbon monoxide poisoning, the county coroner said.

Heaving backs, cascades of shedding tears. We all cried.

We cried because it wasn't possible that Karla and Sonny were gone; it was unbelievable. We cried for the loss of two classmates who, for some of us, had been our friends since early childhood. We cried because it didn't seem real that Karla and Sonny were no longer among the living. We cried because they didn't deserve to die; both were popular and respected, known for their kindness and consideration to all.

We cried.

We cried for Sonny and Karla because they could no longer cry for themselves. We cried because we thought it unfair that two healthy, beautiful and joyous 18-year-olds should die so young. Like so many of us, they were bold and carefree and loved the spotlight, but would experience it no more. We cried for the sadness of the two of them no longer being able to love each other; their dreams included a life together.

We cried.

We cried having lost our innocent belief that we were immortal—could death happen to us? We cried out of fear of the possibility of losing the boyfriend or girlfriend we had, or wished we had.

We cried because it was too sad to watch friends and classmates weeping, most especially those among us who were brazen and unfazed by life's challenges, but who now were devastated. The good and the bad, the hip and the hoodlums, we classmates all cried.

And cried.

We cried because the dead children's parents were so overcome with grief and could find no way to conceal it. In watching their pain we somehow knew that the loss of one's own child is more tragic than any of us could ever comprehend, and that was a frightening perspective. We cried for their loss; we were unable to locate the bottom of our own despair, so we knew we couldn't fathom the depth of theirs.

We cried because our parents were crying; seeing their grief made them more vulnerable than we cared to believe possible. It made us uncomfortable that our protectors, guardians, pillars of strength, caretakers and wielders of privileges could be brought to their knees. This was frightening and so heightened the loss we were all feeling, and so added to our own sorrow.

And so we cried some more.

We cried because the compassion in the room was all-powerful, and we were all so fragile. In every moment an adult or child moved beyond his or her own heartache and reached out to console a loved one, the passion emitted was as heart-wrenching as it was heart-soothing. Fingers eagerly searched out and quickly found companionship with other fingers and intertwined in a desperate grip; a hand unsteadied by grief would grope for the clutch of another hand; a caretaking arm would drape itself around a nearby shuddering shoulder, now stooped in defeat; an arm would wrap itself around a nearby waist. So many sensitive and tender gestures, making even more obvious the value of what we had lost.

The sadness overwhelmed my senses to the point of feeling numb.

Grief.

There seemed to be no way to escape the billions of feelings that demanded reckoning.

Overloaded, my heart needed respite and so intellect switched on and took over. Could we make sense of this? Could meaning be found? Was there even one logical reason to justify this? Hundreds of questions raced through me.

How is it possible that my friends are gone? What will it be like to ride the bus without Karla sitting in the seat beside me? How could I provide leadership at the Future Teachers of America without my vice president at my side? Didn't Sonny sit next to me in the auditorium in the school pep assembly just three days ago? What would I do with the love note that was still in my notebook, the note Sonny had given me to pass on to my friend?

How could I ever forget Karla and Sonny?

The questions raced on.

How could their families make sense of this? And overcome it? How many times will they awaken from their sleep or be distracted from their work with thoughts of their children? How often will the parents rehash the "If only I had said 'no' to my child when he (or she) asked for permission to go out"? Will one parent place blame on the other? Will these deaths bring parents closer, or pull them apart?

What if the last words were of reprimands for a room not cleaned, chores not done, a prank just discovered? How will these parents cope when looking in their children's rooms and closets, seeing and touching their children's belongings? What will their thoughts be as they see photos of their children? Will the photos be taken down from the walls and put away? Will the photos now being displayed in their homes rest in the same place forever?

How will these parents soothe the brothers and sisters when their own grief is so enormous? Will the emptiness of the loss these parents feel ever be filled up? What will fill the void? Will these parents ever remove from their mind's eye the image of their children's youth and vigor and the life force they had come to know from these two young adults, ever so ready to venture out into the world? So many years of parenting; weren't these parents looking forward to their children going forward in life independently, each filled with a dream and aspirations to actualize?

Do these parents envision their child in heaven? How will each parent retain his or her faith in God? Regain equilibrium and go on?

The questions wouldn't quit coming.

How is it possible that those so young can die? What is death like? Is it painful? Is it a relief? Is it wonderful? Does God have control over things like this? How can a loving God take away those so needed by us all? How can those so beautiful, so filled with life, so admired, so needed by all of us, be taken away? If these deaths were accidental, why didn't God save them from death—didn't Sonny and Karla have things yet to do on earth? Didn't they have much left to learn, to do, to see?

And *still* the questions came.

Why an open casket to show everyone a dead life? Why don't they look like themselves lying in those caskets? What's different about their faces? They look so empty. Where is their perpetual aura of joy that hovered around them and could be felt by all? Where are their souls now? From "dust to dust" the minister had said: How long would it take for the fullness of their exquisite youth to become dust? Then what? What will become of their souls. Were their souls here in this room right now, were Sonny and Karla watching us? Did they know this would be their fate? Was it predestined? Had Sonny and Karla really chosen early death as their destiny? If so, why? What was the point, the lesson, the teaching?

A funeral is a ritual to bring closure, completion, finality. Why, then, did our grieving go on?

Everyone in the community, it seemed, knew we children couldn't deal with the range and inconsistency of the feelings we were experiencing. Many of the adults found solace in God and in each other. We children just wanted our friends to wake up from their deaths and get on with our lives. Finals were around the corner; how could we study without them? The season with the best of the school activities was soon under way. How would we do these without them?

Perhaps it was from experience that the adults in the community knew they needed to rally around the children to help us overcome the enormous emptiness we were feeling. Or perhaps it's just the way small communities reach out to others in times of need. Whatever the reason, people everywhere became a part of our healing.

From bedroom to boardroom to classroom, the entire community rallied around; healing the community's children became a group effort. We children were soothed by voices of kindness, and by hands—numerous ones, resting on our heads, shoulders, backs, actions intended to soothe the young—that assisted us in our healing. Kindness was offered as medicine, and so we swallowed it.

"How are you, Bettie?" Mrs. Houck, the drugstore clerk, asked. She had helped me before, but not with such extraordinary concern.

"That might be tough to locate; let me help you," said Mrs. Tarcher, the all-too-busy and overworked librarian with the policy of making students locate resources themselves.

"How are you doing, Miss Burres?" asked Mr. Thomas, a retired postal worker with a reputation as a rather quiet and keep-to-yourself gentleman. He stopped in the middle of the sidewalk and, searching my face, was interested in getting a response to his question. For several years I had waved to this man as he drove away from the daily mail delivery, but I had never actually spoken to him before.

"How may I help you?" the postal clerk asked, even more kindly than usual.

"No homework tonight" was said daily by all teachers for nearly a week.

For the next several months every educator, support staff person and administrator stood in the school halls to greet all children, making a point to look directly at us and to address each of us by name. Now teachers got up from their desks more often, walking between the rows of students' desks, taking the time to linger a bit by each of our desks. Boxes of tissues were placed near the edge of the teacher's desks and on more than one occasion, it was the teacher who delivered the tissue to a teary-eyed student.

Classroom aides or those who normally didn't have a reason to be closely involved with the students, now touched our hands and shoulders and made eye contact as often as possible. Sincere smiles were abundant from everyone.

The practice of one student going to the teacher's desk each day to get the roll book, and after calling out each student's name, marking attendance by placing a "P" for present or an "A" for absent, ended abruptly. Now the teacher took roll silently, no doubt to help ease the remembering of the deaths and noticeable absence of our two beloved classmates. When John Hansen's family moved out of the community, his empty desk was moved to the back of classrooms. Karla and Sonny's desks, now empty, disappeared from the classrooms entirely.

Healing.

Soon the questions in our minds slowly transformed from "Why did this happen?" to "How can we find courage?" It was time for recovery.

The little town in the middle of the nation that endorsed the African proverb, "It takes an entire village to raise a child," had successfully rallied around their children. The community helped its children cope with their pain, deal with it day by day, and when it was deemed that their children were ready to move beyond grief, helped their young restore their faith in God and learn to see death as a stage of life. Death, though final, wasn't final, but rather, another stage of life. And so joy became an option.

And so it was that we were able to remember Karla and Sonny as the vibrant and beautiful people they were, and draw strength from the love and joy they had so freely shared with us. Our comments changed from "Remember . . ." to "This one's for

Karla (or Sonny)!" Their lives didn't have to be forgotten, nor our needs to remember them; our feelings didn't have to be shrouded in denial. Karla and Sonny could be remembered with joy.

So we dedicated the class yearbook to our friends, and in it we wrote, "In Memoriam—to Karla and Sonny—He who is dead and gone, honor with remembrance, not with tears."

Sonny and Karla were mentioned in the high school graduation commencement speech that sunny Sunday afternoon, renewing for us their absence. Some of us, it appeared, had saved a few tears for this honoring; all of us wished they were here with us. "They're here in spirit," our class president reassured us.

Perhaps it was just coincidence—or a heart's prerogative to choose its own course of action—that when the ceremony ended, a hundred-plus joyous graduates looked at each other and, without speaking words, in unison flung our caps wildly into the air with the chant, "To Sonny and Karla!" Just as joyously, we grabbed from the air any available hat falling that landed either in our hands or near our feet and then raced off to the auditorium to return the rented caps and gowns.

Mr. Scholton wasn't all that happy that two caps were missing.

Then the custodian of some 30 years walked in carrying two graduation caps. "Found these two laying on top of the old basketball hoop," he said in his usual helpful manner. "Practically on top of each other, kinda like they were hiding." Chuckling, he added, "Maybe they just didn't want the moment to end."

For many of us, in our minds, this peculiar incident was symbolic of something more. Our class president had been right. Sonny and Karla *were* with us.

We graduates were silent as we left the auditorium that day—many of us far wiser than we knew.

18

Norm and Norma

"I will help you," the little boy said, reaching for Norma's tiny hand and placing it in his own. "And I won't let anyone laugh at you no more." We watched, awed by his skills of compassion—uncommon, we thought, for one as young as us.

It was the first day of kindergarten. Too shy to ask the teacher to use the bathroom, and too timid to use it without first getting permission, five-year-old Norma sat at her small desk crying because she had wet herself.

It wasn't long before all the other students heard her soft whimpers and began staring in her direction. Some students laughed because they thought her predicament funny; others

*Excerpted from *Helping Kids Cope with the Stress, Strains, and Pressures of Life*, New York: Random House, 1995, Dr. Bettie B. Youngs, Ph. D., Ed. D.

giggled, no doubt out of relief that it had happened to her and not to them. But one brave little boy did not laugh. Instead, Norm got up from his desk, walked over to his classmate and looking at her, said softly, "I will help you." We were all sitting and he was standing, so his presence seemed almost majestic. "And I won't let them make fun of you," he said reassuringly.

My tiny classmate looked up at Norm and smiled with admiration. His act of kindness had buffered her duress; she no longer felt afraid and alone. She had found a new friend.

Still holding her small hand, the little hero turned, surveyed his classmates and asked kindly, "How would you feel if it happened to you?" The wise teacher at the head of the classroom observed quietly, but said nothing.

We children sat motionless, stilled partly by the enormous strain and anxiety caused by the drama in this moment, but also because we had just witnessed an act of heroism we had not been able to summon in ourselves. It was a lesson in how precious goodness can be.

Then the little boy added, "Let's not laugh at her anymore, okay?" Intuitively, we knew we were in the presence of courage.

And by his actions, we were persuaded to develop some of our own.

19

Free Speech

"Dad said no, that stupid jerk!"

I didn't expect to be slapped. And so sharply!

I was throwing a tantrum, the kind typical of 14-year-olds who have been told "No" by a parent and *understand* fully that the no means no!

"But I'll die if I can't go . . ."

"Somebody else will dance with the boy I like . . ."

"All my friends are going . . ."

"All the kids will think . . . I . . . I . . . I . . ."

I had tried every possible angle of persuasion on my father, but his answer was still a resounding "No!"

Realizing that pleading my case with him was useless, I decided to take my case to the president of second chances—Mom. Surely she would see that Dad had been an ogre in his decision and get him to see how unfair he had been to me. She had all the clout in the world with him; when their discussion was over, I would be going to the dance!

"And Dad said no, that . . ."

That's when my mother reached out to get my attention. "Don't you ever, ever say that about your father," she warned.

I couldn't believe Mom's response. Dad had said "No!" to my going to the most important school function of the century. I had expected her to understand, and to be on my side. Mom knew how important it was to me that I be allowed to attend *the* school dance. I wanted her to say, "I'll talk to your father and see if I can get him to change his mind." After all, Mom was used to intervening for her children, and pretty successfully, too.

Instead, she said, "I want you to understand that you will *not* speak like that about your father. Speaking that way about your dad is disrespectful. Do you understand?"

I nodded in agreement. Softly now and very respectfully I begged, "But Mom, you *have* to get him to say yes."

"That's another issue," Mom said. "Right now I want you to understand that you are accountable for what comes out of your mouth." She looked at me for a long moment; the silence was painful. Finally she asked, "Who do you consider your best friend among all the girls you know?"

I could see I was in for a lecture; at this point I wanted to make sure that it was only a verbal one, so I decided to be as compliant as possible.

"Karla," I said.

"How do you feel when someone puts down your friend?"

"Pretty awful," I said honestly. "It makes me feel bad, sometimes mad."

"Yes," Mom responded, still looking at me intently. "Your dad is *my* best friend. No one will be permitted to put him down in my presence. Being disrespectful to your father is also being disrespectful to me."

It had not occurred to me that respect encompassed the boundaries of the listener as well as the person being talked about. I had violated my mother's loyalty and respect for her friend, her husband.

When Mother understood that I finally understood, she pulled me close to her and said, "I'm very sorry for slapping you. I love you very much. That you learn to treat others with respect is important to me. I want it to be important to you, too. You must learn to express your thoughts clearly and with integrity." With one hand she stroked my hair and with the other hand, wiped away tears now trickling down my cheeks.

"I'm sorry, Mom," I said, crying softly.

We stood with our arms around each other for a moment longer. I resigned myself to the idea that I would be at home on the night all my friends were at the school dance. "I guess this means I won't be going the school dance, huh?" I said with a big sigh.

She moved me away from her so that she could look into my eyes. "Maybe. But maybe not," she said lovingly. "A flower gives off its sweetest fragrance when it's been crushed." She smiled and walked away.

It was a sweet victory. And the best school dance I ever attended!

A Family Tree

20

Whack! One swift blow with the razor-sharp knife was all it took for the old man to hack off the head. It now lay on a huge gnarly root of the old oak tree that doubled as a chopping block on occasions such as this.

There were nearly 20 finger-like roots that clawed at the ground and with a powerful grip, anchored the enormous tree deep within the earth, visibly displaying for all to see its mighty, self-important intentions to exist. From this gigantic tree— whose belly was so big around that it took five children with arms stretched to fully encircle it—sprang seven enormous limbs, each one reaching well into the sky to suck in the sun and air. Each limb was, itself, the size of a mature tree, possessing an ample supply of strong healthy branches. The sheer physical size of the branches made it easy for them to withstand the hardships of the summer's wind and hail storms, and to endure the burden of thousands of heavy icicles in the winter season. Smaller branches sprouted from the bigger branches, all producing lush green foliage in the spring and summer. After painting its leaves in rich gold, amber, sienna brown and orange in the fall, the tree shed them, covering the ground with a foot or more of fallen leaves as though to cover its toes to protect them from the cold.

It was and is simply a grand and majestic tree, a hardy symbol of life, a haughty symbol of strength. But the tree is more. From the beginning of its own life to the present, it has stood watch over the Burres clan's comings and goings; the tree harbors their history. And a busy history at that. Through the years, many events have taken place there.

The old man had a special relationship with the tree. His father had planted it in 1854 on the very day the Burres family staked claim to the rich soil in Humboldt County, Iowa—just a mere few years after the original settler came to this vast prairie land. This piece of land had been but prairie and forest then, home to hundreds of native American eagles. The city two miles away was appropriately named Eagle's Grove by the band of Sioux Indians, later shortened to Eagle Grove.

For the old man, the tree represented more than a commemorative day of a family beginning its history and family life in this location; it was also the beginning of his own history. He was born on the very day the tree was planted. Perhaps that's why he felt such a kinship to the tree. To him, the tree was a family journal. In this spot, people and events stood for something. It was here, under the old oak tree, where elders gathered to commiserate, to sip lemonade on a hot summer's day, to court, to husk corn, to clean fish. Working or playing, it was the central meeting place, or as the old man told it, the gathering place where decisions of consequence—where to get "baptized, married or buried"—were made.

Over the years, the oak tree both celebrated and grieved for family milestones. The old folks rumored that great-grandmother had buried a stillborn child beside this tree (and as the story goes, grew its widest root to shield this sacred spot); my grandfather had married under this glorious tree; aunts and uncles and cousins had baptized their children under it; my father and his cousins as children had played in its colossal limbs, as did their children. We, too, grew up with this oak tree in our presence. We hung makeshift swings from several of its branches, we rescued cats who had climbed too high and we fertilized its roots by burying a beloved dog next to it. As young lovers, my grandparents, aunts, uncles and parents all etched their and their loved one's initials into the bark. As others had done before us, my brothers and sisters and I carved our initials in it, too, and accepted kisses from lovers, some of whom would marry into our growing family. Maybe as a sign of the times or a woman's prerogative to change her mind, my daughter returns each summer and updates her love life's status with a new set of initials, JLY + DB; JLY + BE; JLY + SG. The tree willingly accepts all these past and new revelations.

The old oak tree had status outside the family as well. For travelers coming around the bend from the town of Eagle Grove, the tree is a landmark in reaching their destinations. To the sheep assigned to mow the grass in the large family yard, it is respite from the hot sun.

On this particular day, the old tree watched in approval as one more of the Burres clan members brought the past into the present, and helped the young find meaning and a sense of legacy.

Whack! whack! whack! whack! whack! The old man playfully laughed at the sight of the mutilated bullhead, too small to withstand so many misdirected blows from the heavy, razor-sharp steel fishing knife.

"Here," he said to his great-niece, Judy, laughing. The old man's weathered face was home to a million and one deep lines, each one etched deeper than the next. And a mouth that laughed and talked at the same time.

"Do it like this." Using the sunbass he held in his hand, he showed us how to artfully clean fish. "My father taught me to clean a fish like this . . . like this . . ." he said as he slit the fish down its belly in one swift take and pulled out its guts. In this very spot, right beneath this same old family oak, a father had shown a son; a son had shown his nephew's children.

"Old Uncle Ben," as we called him, was really our great-uncle. He lived with his wife of 50-plus years one mile away on a farmstead that he kept immaculately groomed and manicured. Every week they came bearing gifts—freshly picked fruits and vegetables from their garden, a hand-knit sweater or shawl or doily for Mom, freshly dried tobacco for Dad's pipe, assorted fresh baked cookies or homemade candy for the children.

Like a finely tuned clock, at 2:30 every Sunday afternoon, their old green spit-polished 1939 Chevrolet drove into our yard and parked under the old oak tree, never under the mulberry tree as some guests did (only to return to their car to find that heavy and juice-laden berries had dropped from the tree, leaving a circle of sun-dried purple stains on the car). Out came the folding chairs from the trunk of his car, and he and my father would sit in the yard under the old oak tree and talk; Olga would sit in the old rocking chair in the living room with her blue polka-dot knitting bag at her side, and in between counting the numbers of stitches she was either putting in or taking out, she conversed with our mother.

Just as sure as a clock ticks off one minute after another, at 4:30 the same afternoon, the tall, lean old man and his small hump-shouldered wife would get back into their old green car and drive away as slowly as they had driven in. Every Sunday, without fail. This ritual went on from the beginning of time until I was ten, when Olga died.

It was under the old oak tree that he grieved and mourned his loss. And when he had sufficiently completed his grieving as the head of his family, he lobbied to reposition himself as a contributing member of his nephew's family. "It's about time the kids learn to fish," he earnestly pointed out to my father. Understanding that Old Uncle Ben needed us as much as we needed him, my father and mother agreed. From that day forward, on cloudy days and rainy days, Old Uncle Ben would pull up in his old green Chevy, fishing poles protruding out the back windows, and off to the Humboldt River he would take us to learn to fish *with skill*.

The role of teacher/fisherman/grandfather suited him well.

Reeling the fish to shore had been absolutely thrilling. How patiently I had waited, and waited and waited, watching intently for the little half-red and half-white plastic bobber to move. When finally it did, it bobbed up and down furiously. Ever so silent so as not to scare the fish away, I took the pole with both hands—just as this master with the reputation as the best fisherman in the county had instructed me. Leaning back, I swayed side to side like I had seen Old Uncle Ben do many times, cautiously reeling in this monster of a fish. (Whether this motion helped reel in the fish or was just for show, I didn't know, but I wasn't about to ask.)

At first the enormous fish merely glided through the waters toward me, but as it neared the shore, it jerked and fought me every inch of the way. But I won. The fish flopped one time too many, flopped right out of the water and onto the bank of the river. I dropped my pole, grabbed the big net, flung it over the fish and pounced on it. The prized fish was mine!

"It's *huge!*" screeched my sister, confirming the size of the fish.

"It's soooo beautiful!" I said, hardly believing that I had finally caught a fish. And such an enormous one.

"Sure is," confirmed Old Uncle Ben. "Must be nearly a half pound, that one! Might as well toss him back in, though. Unfortunately, we can't eat him."

"What?" my sister and I groaned in unison. "Why can't we take him home and show him to Mom and Dad and Mark and Kevin and Tim and all the kids at school, and eat him? Why not, Old Uncle Ben? Why not? Pleazzze?"

"Because it's a scavenger fish, and it eats everything in the river," he replied. "You'll get sick if you eat it."

I looked at the beautiful big fish I was cradling, the fish that was now being described as lower than a life form.

I had caught a nothing fish. Worse, I had caught a fish with a bad reputation. As disrespectfully as I could, I kicked that scum bag of a fish into the weeds, and then rigorously rubbed my shoes in the grass to be sure that not one scale or drop of slime from the defective and imperfect fish remained on my shoes.

"From here on out all I want to catch is sunbass," I sulked.

"Not me," said my wonderfully rebellious-as-usual sister Judy, picking up the disregarded carp and putting it in the pail of fish that were worthy of being taken home. "I want to catch a carp bigger than you did."

No sooner had she made this announcement when she yelled, "Hurry, Old Uncle Ben, it's a really *big* one."

He had the patience of a saint. Old Uncle Ben carefully positioned his own pole in the makeshift stand and rushed to my sister's pole. "By golly, that pole has quite a bend in it," he said, looking at the large circle of rippling water around her fishing line. "You must have something." The same moment he reached for her pole the line snapped, and the tire emerging from the river slowly sank out of view. "Oh, my," he laughed merrily. "You caught a Firestone tire. An unusable one, I'm afraid."

Judy and I thought it hysterical, and laughed until we cried. Old Uncle Ben laughed, too, probably because we were laughing.

I noticed that my line was not where I thought I had cast it.

"Old Uncle Ben, Old Uncle Ben," I called out. "Hurry! My worm's going to fall off." Two old, nearly worn-out eyes peered over the brown speckled frames of his thick glasses, the right eye revealing a heavily layered and dense cataract. The better eye followed the line from my pole up into the tree over my head where a juicy earthworm, impaled by the hook, dangled from the tree.

"Okay, I'll be right there," he said, chuckling, not one bit annoyed. "Let me just get a new line and hook and sinker for your sister and I'll be right over." When he had repaired her pole and cast it back into the river, he turned his attention to the messy project I had created.

No sooner had he started to retrieve my line than Judy tossed her pole to the ground, running along the banks of the river to follow the now-freed tire being carried downstream by the current.

"Wait, Judy," he shouted. "You can't leave your pole unattended." No sooner had he warned her than some mysterious force in the water swiftly attacked the worm at the end of her pole and carried it off, taking my sister's pole and all downstream.

Still he took us fishing, again and again, until he had taught us to fish *with skill*.

Old Uncle Ben had shown us how to catch fish with skill, and insisted we learn to clean them *with skill* as well.

The old man stooped to pick up the head of the fish, now detached from its body, and flung it to the flock of honking geese, all vying for the same piece. With two bloody and fishy-smelling fingers, he removed the familiar saliva-drenched stub of a tattered and unlit cigar from his mouth and lay it carefully in the arch of the tree branch above his head. He lay the cigar in its resting place, next to the initials BNB + OAC carved inside the shape of a heart. Olga had been his first and only love, and his wife. The sight of the initials made him smile. He gently brushed his fingers over the little heart-shaped love-scar.

"Tell us the story again, Old Uncle Ben," we'd say as we cleaned the day's catch under the big old tree. And he would, telling us again and again his favorite childhood stories, those his mother and father and aunts and uncles and cousins had told him. Story after story. Memory after memory of his family, his boyhood years, his life and times. Old times, and now times.

During those cherished hours, Old Uncle Ben passed on the value and importance of our past. So many generations down the line, and here I was, living on the very homestead my ancestors had settled. Now my parents were farming this rich soil and raising their family here. And the tree was still working, still serving.

Like generations before us, our family, too, worked and played under the tree. In canning season the fruits and vegetables were brought here to be processed, whether it was to husk corn, shell peas, peel apples, wash cucumbers, remove the stems from the yellow and green beans—all was done under the old oak tree. Weekly sacrifices of fowl to the family table, be it a chicken, goose, or duck, were carried out on one of the large knuckle-like shelves that served as a chopping block. Another shelf held the hatchet, imbedded for safety, resting and waiting for its next use. Help hired to assist with the baling of the summer's straw and hay are still served lunch here. Seed corn sales and other farm business are often negotiated there still. As young children, the siblings met under the tree to strategize, to hold "club" meetings and to play. Several of the younger generation of cousins and their lovers have been discovered "petting" there, and my daughter has staked claim to the tree—she has dreams of one day marrying beneath its dazzling arms.

In the Burres family, only the old oak tree knows when one generation ends and the next begins. The tree is our common link; it binds us, one and all, reminding us that we have each been here and endured. Though we have passed through different lifetimes and seemingly different cultures, the proud tree reminds us of our oneness, our legacy, one that is rich in history and culture.

It is a human bond, this tree.

Old Uncle Ben, that splendid old man, died at the age of 82, after all his nephew's children had learned to fish—*with skill*. Perhaps it's not all that coincidental that on the day Old Uncle Ben died, lightning struck the ancient oak tree, causing one of its huge limbs to break off.

We children watched in silence as my father sawed the enormous fallen limb into smaller pieces so that it could be hauled away. As he pulled one large piece away, my sister Judy suddenly shouted, "Stop, Daddy."

She ran to the log and pointed, "Look!" My father looked down at the spot where she had pointed, then walked back to the tractor and turned it off. He then picked up the chain saw and cut out the piece my sister had called attention to. When the piece popped out, he picked it up and, with a thoughtful look on his face, lovingly handed it to my sister. Crying, she carried away a piece of wood wherein an engraved heart carried the initials BNB + OAC.

Some love affairs last *forever*. And some people—like Old Uncle Ben—love in ways that make their love *live* forever.

Mailboxes

The family mailbox stood at the end of the half mile-long lane. In tall, proud white capital letters it announced to all who passed by: BURRES. To us children that metal container on a post was a source of endless anticipation and a source of independence. And a promise of unconditional love.

Our mother had created this sense of adventure for us, probably not inadvertently; children needed to learn things. To Mom, everything was a teachable moment. And she was a master teacher.

Each day, around noontime, my mother would walk down the lane to get the mail. When we children saw her head for the lane on Saturdays, we would drop our activities and scurry to join her, as would the dog member of the family. Mom was a mother who found great pleasure in her children's company, happily and playfully greeting us as we joined her. The half-mile trek to and from the mailbox was a long way for short legs, but well worth it. During these trips, her mood was reliably joyous; this was an opportunity to bask in our mother's love.

Once we arrived at the mailbox, Mom would pick out the mail and while sorting through it, announce if mail had arrived for any of the children—though she wouldn't give out the names of just who among us had received mail. By doing it this way, all of us children were kept in suspense until we had reached the house, at which time we would be given our individual mail. Mother made a point of teaching us to respect each other's privacy, and to be a *very* good sport about who did and did not receive mail on any given day. "Here," she would say, "This belongs to *you*." We were all allowed to open the mail that came in our names without Mom looking over our shoulders.

Surprisingly, each child received mail from time to time. Even more surprisingly, each child received mail in fairly equal quantities. Sometimes a magazine arrived in a child's name, sometimes a note from an aunt, uncle, grandma, grandpa or Sunday school teacher (who was also our neighbor, and Mom's good friend). No child was left wanting. Even junk mail arrived on cue. Written by a person or by a machine, it didn't matter; getting mail with your name on it was exciting and esteeming.

The practice of children getting to open their own mail continued from the day I was old enough to know what mail was, to the day I left home. It wasn't until I was much older that I understood that while we children were caught up in the fun of receiving mail, Mother's strategy held even bigger intentions.

On those brief strolls, Mom would sometimes tell us a story made up to fit the moment; at other times she used it to teach us about God. Sometimes these were the same. Mom used every opportunity to help us become aware of the obvious miracles of God's creation. There wasn't a bird or bee, flora or fauna that went unnoticed. To her, everything was evidence of God's love and involvement in the world. The fascinating habits of animals on the ground or in the air, which ones are dangerous and which aren't, and how God gave those "dangers" to animals for their protection; the intricacy and beauty in the colors and shapes and fragrances of flowers; how the bees fly to them to gather their pollen; the sun with its endless power and brilliance to warm and give light, all were pointed out to us for appreciation.

We adored her. She was our everything. This was a joyous woman, an eternal optimist, always smiling, always humming, her words punctuated with an easy flowing laughter that caused her long, soft brown hair to be tossed over her shoulders. She was a beautiful and feminine woman with blue eyes and flawless skin, her hour-glass figure always adorned in a flower print dress. We never questioned her love for us, or her unwavering faith in the power of God and his ability to intervene in our daily lives.

One day she spoke to us about the power of prayer. "Praying is like sending a letter," Mother said. "You have to formulate your thoughts, send them to God, and then wait for a reply."

"Does God *always* answer prayers?" Judy questioned.

"Oh, yes," Mom said with easy certainty. "All you need to do is ask God for help, and God will answer you. The answer may not always be yes, but you will get an answer."

Going for clarification, Judy asked, "Even if you are bad?"

"Yes," Mom answered.

"What if it's a *really* big request?" bantered Judy.

"With God's help," Mom replied, "nothing is impossible."

Hearing the reverence in Mom's voice, I knew she was telling us the truth.

"How do you know if your prayer is answered?" I asked.

"Because a miracle will happen," Mom explained. "You will see a sign, or *feel* the answer inside."

"Where do you feel it?" I asked.

"You will hear the answer in your heart," responded Mom.

"How does your heart *hear*?" I asked.

"It's a certain feeling you get. For me, it's a warm sensation that I feel right here in my chest," she said, placing her hand over her heart.

"How does it feel if God says no?" I asked.

Placing her hand on my shoulder for reassurance, she said, "I trust that whatever the answer is, God thinks it's the right one *for me*, and I thank God for helping me find the *best* way to do something."

As was my mother's habit, once the mail had been gathered, her attention turned to gathering flowers. She loved flowers and planted them along the fence line in the lane and around the mailbox. A wild and colorful assortment of sunflowers, African daisies, bachelor buttons, Indian blankets, bluebells, poppies, Texas bluebonnets, impatiens and zinnias bloomed in wild abandon. Magically she would capture the essence of each day's journey, as she used the scissors she always carried on these trips to snip a bouquet of her favorite flowers along the way. In the early spring she would sometimes carry a small kitchen knife to pluck the fresh asparagus that grew abundantly in the fence line of the lane. After she had cut flowers she would call out, "Okay, let's journey home." This was our cue to turn homeward.

I thought a lot about what my mother had taught me that particular day, not realizing I would put her words to the test so soon. The idea of not only talking to God, but also being able to ask for His help if I needed it, was a powerful concept to me, and I took it quite literally.

The following day I came across small insects scurrying about their daily business. I was amazed by the strong-man feats of a trail of ants carrying huge loads in comparison to their tiny frames, up into the hole at the top of their ant hill. As I watched, I was distracted by something going on out of the corner of my eye. I turned and saw it struggling on the ground. He was beautiful, but I knew he was in trouble and something inside told me he needed my help. He was a plump, fuzzy, black and yellow bumblebee, about the size of a baby hummingbird. I tenderly scooped him up into the palms of my small hands, tightly cupped together, providing him a safe shelter. He fluttered and buzzed faintly inside my grasp. Even in my youth I could tell that he was sick and possibly dying, and I knew if anyone could make him well, my mother could. She had repaired and nursed many a wounded child, bird and animal back to health. I ran to the house with the bee. When I opened up my cupped hands to let my mother examine her newly found patient, the look on her face was one of alarm.

"Bettie, that bumblebee might sting you, put it down!" she said firmly.

"No, Mom, he's sick. We have to help him," I pleaded. My mother took a closer look at the bee and observed the tiny creature's legs just barely moving.

"Honey, God's the only one who can help that bee now. He's almost dead."

"But Mom," I pleaded, "there has to be something we can do!"

"I'm afraid not," Mom said.

"But we can't let him die!" I cried. "You said flowers need the bees, so we can't let him just die, Mom. There must be something we can do."

"It's nature's way, honey," Mother said, searching for words of comfort. "Take him outside. Bury him if you want."

I slowly walked with my dying bee to the large oak tree in our yard and sat under its protective branches. Sitting on one of its large finger-like roots, I leaned back on the tree's enormous trunk. My mind raced, searching for another alternative, and then I remembered my mother's words: "With God's help, nothing is impossible." I closed my eyes tightly and bowed my head, and with my hands still cupped around the bee, I prayed to God with the simple faith of a child.

"Dear God," I prayed, "this bumble bee is very sick and my mom said You are the only one who can help him, so please fix him. Amen."

Not sure what to do at that point, I remained still to allow God the time he needed. That's when God worked the miracle. And I felt it. A soothing feeling welled up inside of me, and I knew this to be the feeling my mother had talked about, the one where she said her heart can "hear." God was answering my prayer.

I slowly allowed one eye to open and then the other, and looked down at my closed cupped hands. I cautiously opened my fingers, one at a time, and looked at the bee.

Whoosh! The bee swiftly flew from my grasp. At first the bee flew only a short distance and then took a nose dive to the soft grass below. But the bee rested for only a moment before it took flight again. Then, right before my eyes, I watched as the bumblebee disappeared out of sight.

"God," I screeched in amazement. "You did it! You really did it. You fixed the bee!"

Remembering that Mom had said you need to thank God, I quickly squeezed my eyes closed and said, "Thank you, God."

It was a very happy revelation. I rushed to the house and told my mother what had happened. To my surprise, she acted dismayed. To reassure her, I said, "It happened just like you said it would. I asked God for help and He did."

That sweet familiar smile crossed my mother's face, and she said, "Yes sweetheart, miracles do happen."

And so it is that the sight of mailboxes, especially those at the end of long lanes, retains special meaning for me. They remind me of my mother's love and the values and beliefs she so lovingly conveyed; she embodied joy, love and respect; she taught joy, love and respect.

Always mailboxes remind me of my mother's love for her children—then and now. Her love for her children was from the heart, and she found it a duty to instill in us a faith in God—a God that was a loving and benevolent father, one who joyfully, lovingly and respectfully played with all His creatures daily.

Mailboxes also symbolize my personal connection to God, and the "correspondence" that joyfully, lovingly and respectfully goes on between us—one that my heart readily "hears."

While I no longer naively believe that God can fix all dying bees, I do know that God permeates all things. Through God all things are possible. I know that all prayers, large and small, are answered. And that if you will be still, you will "hear" God answer.

Little did I know then, that on the ritual journey down the lane to the mailbox, my mother was teaching the most important lesson of all—it was about correspondence with God, and the journey home. Home, to God.

22

Oh, for Boys Like This . . .

Mostly he wore blue denim shirts over very broad shoulders and divinely muscled arms with bulging veins the size of coils. And tight Levi jeans that followed every subtle move he made. Lush tousled hair, the smell of Kouros, a self-assured stand, a confident strut. Sparkling eyes and a generous warm smile that conveyed much more than his words.

Oh for boys like this, with strong healthy bodies . . . and wit and intellect to match. Boys who know the names of wildflowers in the meadows and frequently pick you bouquets. Boys who can locate the constellations in the galaxy; can tell the difference between a cumulus and cirrus cloud, between mist and fog, between a red roan filly and a chestnut gelding, between the chirp of a cricket and a cicada; can distinguish from a distance an eagle from a hawk; can tell the time by raising their eyes to the sky. Oh, for boys like this . . . who know how to treat you to a night on the town in style; invite you on Sunday afternoon picnics in the park and walks in the rain; who take you fishing happily (and bait your hook), swimming in the streams, and horseback riding in the meadows. Oh for boys like this . . . who know the words to the hymns in church and can sing along to George Straight, too; who open doors for babies and ladies and old men, too. Boys who hold you like they mean it. Who do wet kisses. And who listen and understand when you need it.

Off I went with such a boy, learning the meaning of spontaneity, smelling the scent of wildflowers in the meadows, locating the stars in the night's sky, warming my bare legs in the sun, naming clouds, counting eagles, packing picnics, picking wild berries, returning his lingering wet kisses. Oh, for boys like this.

Oh . . . for boys like this . . .

Boys in the heartland are like this.

23

Newark #7

The walk down the half-mile lane was fine, but the next two-mile hike to the little country school was arduous and downright exhausting. My sister Judy and I made this trip twice daily, on foot—our own! Being kids, we complained and considered this akin to child abuse, but of course our parents chalked this up to good exercise.

At the end of this two-and-half-mile journey sat Newark #7. That was our school. Not Woodrow Wilson School or Thomas Jefferson School or Abraham Lincoln School, just Newark #7. Newark #7 was a little white schoolhouse sitting on two acres of tree-lined property complete with a sandbox, six swings and a baseball diamond. The school was the day-home to 16 kinder-garten through twelfth-grade students. My first five years of school life were spent here. The cast of characters at Newark #7 was an assortment of colorful personalities. Every day was a crash course in relationships, and communal living at its best and worst. In addition to these lessons, there was much to be learned from the clever leadership offered by Mrs. Hood and the way she ran the school. My Newark #7 experience accounts for some basic beliefs I still hold today about the nature of people, organizations and life.

Mrs. Hood was not only our teacher; she was counselor, nurse, coach, principal, artist and musician-in-residence, psychologist and mother-of-the-day, every day. She was a nurturing woman and a good educator who genuinely liked her students, every one of them, which is more than I could say. I wasn't particularly fond of Carolyn Brown or Larry Denkclaw. Like all the other students, I really liked Mrs. Hood.

For a long time we thought that Mrs. Hood was somebody really famous because the teacher in the picture that hung adjacent to the fire extinguisher and just above the tornado evacuation instructions looked exactly like her. But MaryLou Mericle told us it was not Mrs. Hood, that it was just a magazine cover by a famous painter named Norman Rockwell. We didn't believe MaryLou until she proved it by pointing to the headline on the print that read, *The Saturday Evening Post*, March 17, 1956, 15¢. In the photo the woman wore a white blouse with a rounded collar and a brooch, and a long full gray skirt and loafers. So did Mrs. Hood. Only her hair was different. Mrs. Hood wore her shoulder-length hair flipped up, but the woman in the photo wore her hair drawn back in a little bun and secured with a white ribbon. It was obvious to me, no matter what anyone else said, that Mr. Rockwell knew Mrs. Hood.

Every school has its status symbols and Newark #7 was no different. Here the hard wooden desk took top marks. Each desk had a little groove that held one eraser and one pencil, no more and no less. And a student, according to size. The smallest children sat in the first rows, the taller and bigger children sat in the back, and other body sizes sat in between. The desks in the back of the room always had the most fun!

Aside from the who's who list, to have a desk or not to have a desk played a part in defining a student's role in the school hierarchy. A desk of your own had to be earned, and carried with it a responsibility to keep it clean inside and out, and above all, to keep it free of any free-floating used gumballs that might want to attach themselves to the underside. Under Mrs. Hood's direction, students conducted a gumball check every morning, right after reciting the Pledge of Allegiance.

We kept our desks, these prize possessions, neat and orderly and in scrupulously straight rows. If you didn't take care of your desk, or if you for some reason weren't considered a student "in good standing," you could lose your desk privileges. If that occurred, you shamefully took a seat at the big wooden table in the back of the room. This was to be avoided at all costs, not only because it was too cold to sit there in the winter and too hot in the fall, but because all of your books, papers and school supplies had to be placed on top of the table, and that was a real inconvenience. Plus, sitting alone at the table with your back to the rest of the students meant missing out on all the goings-on, and that was no fun either.

Aside from the classroom, there were only three other rooms in the schoolhouse—the bathroom, the cloakroom and the basement. The basement had a number of functions, the first being that it served as a safety shelter should a tornado come twisting through the area, which happened from time to time. When it rained or snowed, the basement became the recess playground. Most of the games were great fun, except for the game of Pin-the-Tail-on-the-Donkey. I found this game terrifying. Blindfolded children were given a safety pin and a piece of paper in the shape of a donkey's tail and told to locate the right person and pin it on that person. I just knew that someone, most notably Larry Denkclaw, was going to stick me with a pin—on purpose. I made a promise to God that if I didn't get stuck, I wouldn't throw Carolyn's purse in the toilet, even if she kept on copying my papers. That's how I learned that God answers prayers for sure because I never once was stuck, although every now and then someone else was.

The third use was for "time-out"—a rare occurrence, though from time to time a student taxed Mrs. Hood's saintly patience beyond all hope. Being sent to the basement, besides being a disgrace, could be scary until you reached the long dangling string used to pull on the light, especially after Mrs. Hood had read that story about a troll who hid out under bridges and dark places, like basements, and ate children. I was more than a little vague about the anatomy of a troll and too embarrassed to ask what one was. Larry Denkclaw said a troll was sort of an ugly gigantic spider the size of a skunk complete with very long, hairy legs with poisonous claws at the end of them, and it liked to live in dark secluded spaces, preferably near doorways. He said he had seen one in the basement once, just biding its time until some unsuspecting child came along and it could suck out all her blood. I made sure that whenever I was going to the basement, I was behind someone bigger and stronger than I was. That way, I figured, the troll would naturally go for the other person first. No way was I going to be sacrificed to The Troll!

The tiny cloakroom was home to sweaters, coats, scarves, hats, boots, gloves and lunch boxes. Immediately next to the cloakroom was the bathroom, or the toilet room, as all the kids called it. Since it was necessary to pass through the cloakroom to get to the toilet, we children always kept an eye on who was on his or her way there because every now and then something would turn up missing from the cloakroom. We especially kept an eye on Larry Denkclaw, because his lunch box had a reputation for occasionally containing a swiped cookie or an apple or a Babe Ruth candy bar from one of the other lunch boxes. On occasion, his lunch box also became transport for small creatures of Larry's choosing, especially grasshoppers, crickets and beetles. Sometimes items nestled in our coat pockets would rather cuddle up in Carolyn Brown's coat pockets. When one of the students had a birthday and brought treats for everyone (a custom), there would inevitably be a shortage, so you can see how important it was that we monitor the toilet traffic.

The only thing in the toilet room was the toilet and a sink that no one could reach until they in were in eighth grade or sat near the back of the room. The toilet was a huge open-faced, bottomless, black tunnel-like hole that disappeared deep into the bowels of the earth. As an added touch of intimidation, the mouth of this toilet was so big around that if you weren't holding on to the all-too narrow rim of that seat with both hands and with all your might, there was a good chance that you would fall in. If you did, you would disappear forever, so it was especially important to jump down from this monstrosity *before* you flushed it. Watching the water swirl around and around and down was scary, almost as scary as the sound it made in the process. Pulling the flush lever resulted in an enormous growl, whereby the jowls of this thing released gallons of water that were ferociously inhaled and then sucked down into oblivion. This deep dark mysterious abyss was rumored to have snakes in it, and so became the locus of control for many pranks and a few threats—some made good. Larry Denkclaw threatened to push Steve Mericle down there because Steve refused him double birthday treats, and I once told Carolyn Brown that if she didn't stop copying my spelling papers I was going to throw her purse in.

When Larry Denkclaw told everyone that he had kissed my sister, his rubber galoshes disappeared the same day. At first it was rumored that the troll had stolen Larry's rubber galoshes and taken them into the basement, but that story was dispelled the next day when Danny Thompson convinced Larry that he had seen one of Larry's boots floating downstream when he and his father were fishing from the banks of the Des Moines River the same evening his galoshes were missing.

Presumably, the only way Larry's boots could have landed in the river was by way of the toilet. Larry was sure the culprit was my sister Judy, and so planned his revenge. The next day, after we all had recited the Pledge of Allegiance, Larry reached into his coat pocket and gingerly pulled out a small feather with a fine thread tied to the end. Sitting behind the unsuspecting Judy, he slipped the tiny feather down the back of her dress. As Mrs. Hood read the morning's assignments, Judy leaped to her feet screaming something was crawling on her. Larry released the thread and when Mrs. Hood asked Judy if she was alright, Judy, embarrassed by her display, sat down and said whatever it was must be gone. I was relieved because I had been trying to get Judy's attention, but to no avail. Mrs. Hood continued reading aloud. Larry once again pulled the thread and Judy once again leapt to her feet screaming, clawing frantically at her back. Mrs. Hood came over to investigate but did not notice the thread. She told Judy that there was nothing there, and one more outburst would result in a five-minute time-out in the basement.

Larry's plan was working perfectly. Just as Mrs. Hood and the entire class finally settled into a false sense of security, Larry struck his final blow, sending Judy running up the aisle and Mrs. Hood over the edge. An exasperated Mrs. Hood directed the still-screaming Judy to the basement door.

Judy, doing an "ants in her pants" dance and already in a state of panic, her mind flooded with the vision of the ugly troll, took her first steps downward. She groped for the dangling string at the bottom of the stairs, pulled downward and heard a faint click, but there was no light. She tugged again and again and still no light. As she stood trembling at the bottom of the dark staircase, a creature darted past her, brushing its hairy body against her leg as it scampered across the room.

Horrified, Judy darted up the stairs with speed any Olympian would be proud of. Her cotton dress caught the door handle, ripping from the waistline to the hemline, but she kept going. The class all turned toward the commotion and shrieks, just in time to see Judy emerge hysterically screaming about the troll chasing her, white as ghost. Judy's arms flew around Mrs. Hood, crying hysterically and shaking with fright.

Suddenly the basement door slowly creaked open. Wide-eyed, every student looked in the direction of the basement stairwell. The entire class was absolutely stunned. Even Mrs. Hood didn't know quite what to make of it. Was there really a troll living in the basement after all? Had it really attacked Judy, nearly tearing her skirt off her? Everyone froze, paralyzed, knowing that what attacked Judy was now coming for us all. Mrs. Hood took a step back and held her breath. Judy, still clutching Mrs. Hood, stopped crying and looked over her shoulder at the door, just in time to see a small squirrel run up the stairs, dash across the room and scamper right out the open schoolhouse door.

"Does anyone know how the squirrel got into the basement?" Mrs. Hood asked calmly.

All eyes turned to Larry, who revealed his entire revenge plot. Cleverly, Larry had concealed a little squirrel in his lunch box and, sneaking into the basement before school began, released it there. He then partially unscrewed the lightbulb from the socket and returned unnoticed to the playground.

I followed my sister into the cloakroom where she put her coat on over her torn dress. Within moments a pale and somber Stevie Quick came in. He walked to the corner of the room to where last year's textbooks were stacked in boxes. Carefully, he lifted up two boxes and removed Larry's galoshes from where he had hidden them two days earlier in the third box.

"I'm sorry, Judy," he said, paying penance for his part in her ordeal. "Here are Larry's boots. I was angry with him for taking more than his share of my birthday cake, so I was going to take his boots until it was his birthday and he had to give *me* double treats." He picked up the boots and held them out to her. "Here are his boots; I'll give them back to him and take the blame for all of this."

"Not so fast," I said, grabbing the galoshes from him. I took those darn galoshes from Stevie Quick and with great force, threw them into the toilet!

To the best of my knowledge, neither Judy or Stevie ever let on that the boots Danny Thompson had seen floating down the Des Moines River could not possibly have been Larry's. Why, his boots were just now making their journey this very day.

All this excitement aside, the primary business of the basement was that it was home to the wood-burning stove and the drinking fountain. Fresh drinking water was needed daily, as was wood for the furnace in the fall, winter and early spring. These commodities were found at the nearest homestead across the road from the school on the Lempke farm.

At Newark #7 it was common practice to participate equally and fully, *period*. Everyone had to pitch in and pull his or her weight. To help us become well-rounded citizens, each Monday of every week Mrs. Hood asked for two volunteers for each day of the week to take on the chores that needed to be done. The funny thing about charity was how it seemed to happen to people in pairs. For example, I felt most charitable when Orval Kinne did. Orval was a big guy, a fatherly character, strong and good-natured, and I looked up to him. He was very pleasant to look at, too! Plus, he would open a door and let me go in first—I really liked that. When Orval and I were assigned to get the day's supply of coal, wood and water, Orval would carry all of it. Better yet, he was content to let me run along at his side to keep him company. I liked that, too. *[Author's Note: Nearly 30 years later, and some 10 cities away, Orval Kinne's grown daughter would meet my sister Judy's grown son, and marry and become parents!]*

Other children had their preferences as well. Everyone raised his or her hands to volunteer when MaryLou did. Larry Denkclaw, who always lusted for my sister (then and all through high school), volunteered when she did. Carolyn Brown, infatuated with Stevie Quick, volunteered when he did. If Carolyn Brown raised her hand first, then no one would volunteer, even when erasing the board was held out as the incentive to find this forlorn child a partner. If Carolyn hadn't been a student at our school, we would have learned to become good citizens sooner.

Fall brought with it bushel baskets of golden yellow, rust and orange-colored leaves. For some reason, Mrs. Hood felt these leaves did not have the right to lie on the ground and so sentenced them to be penned up and burned. Instinctively we knew when we were going to be slaving in the schoolyard instead of toiling at our desks. When the list for getting Good Citizenship marks changed from "Play Yard Cooperation" to "Play Yard Responsibilities," we knew the season for blisters was close at hand. And when potatoes, carrots, onions, string beans, a roll of tin foil, an oven rack and a package of beef from LeRoy's Locker appeared behind Mrs. Hood's desk, we knew the day of drudgery was upon us.

Year to year, fall to fall, the process was the same; the older children were assigned the rakes and a plot of ground to rake, in-between size children were responsible for putting the leaves into the baskets and carrying them to the trash barrel, and younger children received a lesson in meal preparation and outdoor cooking. When the last of the leaves guilty of falling to the ground were impounded and put into the metal trash barrel where they were burned at the stake, the oven rack was placed on the top of the barrel ablaze with leaves, and foil-wrapped lunches were placed on the oven rack and steamed until done. This is not to say that we didn't look forward to this extraordinary culinary delight; this delicious meal had a way of soothing aching back muscles and lessening the burning sting of blisters.

Some children at Newark #7 were more memorable than others; some characters stand out and were absolutely unforgettable, like Orval Kinne. Orval was the oldest student; he was in the tenth grade when I was in second grade. I had a crush on him for years, even after he left the school. Orval was big and strong and liked to teach us how to play sports. Patiently, he taught us to swing the bat at precisely the right moment so that it would connect with the ball, how to spit in your hand just enough so that a fast ball really *was* fast, how to catch a fly-ball or stop a ground ball. He was the best! From him I learned when to sacrifice a hit, how to bunt the ball so it rolled off my bat slowly enough for me to get to first base, how to hit the ball down the baseline when a baseman wasn't in position, how to play first and third base and shortstop, and how to slug the ball over the fence. He was great! And diligent in helping us acquire good skills, which was really saying something, considering that some of the kids were more ignorant of sports than others. Carolyn Brown, for example, thought that a bat was something that hung upside down in dark caves and the World Series was a set of encyclopedias!

MaryLou Mericle was one year younger than Orval and was the prettiest and brightest girl in the school. She was the math whiz kid, so Mrs. Hood enlisted her to help teach mathematics to the other kids. When Mrs. Hood noticed that one student had an easier time of learning a particular subject or skill, that student got to help teach it to his or her peers. At other times, students were given a choice of whom they would like to work with. When Mrs. Hood asked Orval if he needed help with anything, he never said yes unless it was MaryLou who was to be his helper. But if MaryLou was absent from school and Mrs. Hood asked him if he needed help in math, he said no.

While Orval's math intelligence fluctuated with MaryLou's school attendance, his ability to push us high in the swings— higher than anyone else—never faltered. Nor did his charm; a glance at Orval was returned with a wink and smile. Orval was a natural leader and genuinely liked his fellow students. We all had a stake in Orval's education, because when his work was finished, Mrs. Hood would let him take several students at a time outside for recess. On the playground, Orval was king.

If Orval was our unofficial P.E. coach, MaryLou returned the favor when it came to math class. MaryLou Mericle had it all together. She smelled like a gardenia every day. Besides being the Einstein of math, she was the first to complete everything. Sometimes she was smarter than the teacher. If no one had the right answer, Mrs. Hood asked MaryLou because she always knew. And that girl was lucky, too. The barrettes MaryLou wore in her naturally curly hair always matched. You would think she would occasionally lose one of those barrettes, but no, nothing that tragic ever happened to MaryLou. She never struck out at bat, and her tennis shoes never got dirty like the rest of ours did. She always knew when it was going to rain because when we were asked to take off our muddy shoes at the door and go stocking-footed in class, she never once was caught with holes in her socks like the rest of us. The only thing normal about MaryLou was that she had a little brother who was *really* slow to catch on to things. He would sometimes have his sweatshirt on backwards, he always emerged from the bathroom with his zipper down and he never did figure out how to put on his gloves so that all the fingers were in the right holes.

Then there was Larry Denkclaw, a student bored with academics but not with teasing and entertaining his classmates. Out of fear, we respected Larry. He brought girlie magazines to school and placed them in the back of his notebook so he could look at them in class. The boys revered him because those who showed allegiance by laughing at his quips and wisecracks were rewarded by getting to sneak a peak at a page of a forbidden magazine. He had clout with the girls, too, because we were scared of which of us he would single out next. When the teacher wasn't looking,

Larry made hissing sounds to draw attention to himself. Of course we would turn and look. Then he would snicker, point his finger at one of the girls, drop his head to look at the girlie picture hidden in the back of his notebook, then back at his victim of choice, back at the picture, then snicker again. It was obvious he knew something about girls that we girls didn't. With Larry we toed the line. He grew up and now owns just about as much land as does God.

Next in line of noteworthy personalities was Carolyn Brown, a pixie-faced, skinny little girl whose mother made her wear frilly full skirts with hoop skirts beneath, even when it obviously hindered her from learning how to play a decent game of ball and prevented her from hanging upside-down on the jungle gym. Carolyn caught one cold a year that lasted all year long. You knew if Carolyn was coming before she got there by the sound of her swishing hoop skirts. She carried a crocheted purse filled with an odd assortment of prescription drugs and cough drops (and gum), enough to cure a town, if need be. She copied everyone's papers, especially mine, since I was small and skinny too, and sat near the front of the room right next to Carolyn. Aside from her strange and silly mannerisms, Carolyn's claim to fame was that she tried to teach us how to chew gum and suck on cough drops in class without getting caught—though her strategy never worked with Mrs. Hood.

There were an assortment of other personalities at Newark #7, but these made up the central cast of characters. Except, of course, for Larry Lempke. Larry was 18 years old, so he was technically the oldest, yet he was actually the youngest. We all liked him and put up with his peculiar behavior, without judgment. His first claim to fame was his parents. Both were devout Christians, very active in the church and pillars in the community. Their farm was adjacent to Newark #7, and it was the Lempke's from whom we got water, coal and wood for the school. Mr. and Mrs. Lempke were genuinely nice people, were citizens in good standing and immensely loved their only child.

Just as Larry had status because he was their son, the Lempkes got some of their status because they were Larry's parents. We referred to them as Mrs. Lempke, Larry's mother, and Mr. Lempke, Larry's father. From church to community to the schoolhouse, we all knew and liked Larry. Larry had status, carte blanche.

What else made Larry extra special was that he had Down's syndrome, so logically the rest of us children were supposed to be more capable than he. This wasn't always the case. While Larry couldn't always accomplish what the rest of us could, let me tell you, he was really quite a gifted fellow. Aside from being a very loving and happy person, he was *very* social. When he was in his seat working on a project that Mrs. Hood had given him, he would sing at the top of his lungs the one and only song he knew, "Jesus Loves Me." When he wasn't singing, he was talking to himself—basically, he was non-stop chatter.

Larry was always dressed very nicely. Good thing, too, because it helped offset his odd physical features. Larry was tall and gangly, and there wasn't a coordinated bone in his body. When it was his turn to bat, we classmates always gave Larry ten tries to hit the the ball, regardless of how many of them were strikes. No one else in the school had the same privileges. Even then he couldn't hit the ball, so the catcher would throw it into the field and tell Larry to run to first base. Larry, of course, thought the ball went flying into the air because he had hit it and, being delighted that he had, would start off on a run, sometimes randomly around the playground or into the parking lot or down the road to his home! To prevent this, we all pretended to fumble the ball long enough for the pitcher to leave her position and guide Larry to first base. Larry just couldn't get the rules of baseball down. Once Larry was on base, the rest of us continued on with the game, ignoring that play completely! We students understood the importance of Larry's simple joys, and good-naturedly put up with his oddities.

Larry had a long nose, a long chin, a long jaw and a long face-topped with a thick mane of hair with more cowlicks than his head had room for. His trademark were his brown Hush Puppy suede shoes; Larry was so enamored with them that whenever he spotted a picture of a basset hound in a magazine, he cut the picture out and, with Scotch tape, taped it to the heel of one of his shoes! Larry had a complete joy of learning, and he never tired of wanting a stroke of recognition from Mrs. Hood, or from all of us, for that matter. Every few minutes he leaped out of his seat and bounded up to Mrs. Hood for approval and acknowledgment on his latest accomplishment, however simple or trivial it might be. It didn't matter to him that she was immersed in her work correcting papers or intensely involved teaching phonics to a reading group. To this very day, I have never met a person with a healthier self-esteem than this happy, and loved by all, young man.

At Newark #7, mainstreaming was at its best.

School and learning were eventful and fun at Newark #7. We students genuinely were saddened when the little country schools closed (as most of them did in 1960) and we were then bused to city schools in nearby towns.

There were so many simple yet profound lessons learned in that simple little neighborhood school. Luckily, many of the things I learned in this setting have been useful throughout my life—in home life, organizational life and in my love life. Among the things I learned:

- Walking uphill to and from school in the snow can be good for your character. And even better for building endurance and a strong and healthy body.
- A good leader (such as a teacher, mother, President) needs to wear many hats.
- Take pride in the way you do your work (and the way you fulfill your responsibilities).
- All hairy creatures encountered in the dark aren't necessarily harmful.
- Pin-the-tail-on-the-Donkey is overrated.
- God is watching; and answers all prayers.
- Pulling your weight maintains friendships and is good for your self-esteem.
- Volunteer.
- Charity happens to people in pairs. (One gives and one receives.)
- Few things are more soothing than a delicious meal after a hard day's work.
- Orval-, MaryLou-, Stevie-, Judy-, Carolyn- and Larry-type personalities turn up in almost all casts of characters—work or play.
- Handicapped people are people with a different set of gifts.
- In serving others, you also serve yourself.
- Hierarchy and pecking order aren't all bad; they have their benefits.
- Cooperation produces better results than competition.

- Helping others produces feelings of personal accomplishment.
- It takes every able body to make up a good team of baseball or whatever—a group, a family, an organization.
- It can be very useful to coach and mentor others. That way every person is better able to give his or her best efforts, making the whole greater than the sum of its parts.
- A co-ed atmosphere provides a rich perspective and leads to learning acceptance of self and others.
- *Doing* is the art of *being*. *Being* is the best reason for *doing*.
- It's good to take pride in one's possessions; it helps one to value the possessions of others.
- The honor system works.
- It's easier to learn when the teacher respects the learner.
- It's better to teach children than to teach subjects.
- Winning is about cooperation; cooperation results in winning.
- There is joy and fun in discovery.
- Achievement and mastery are good for bolstering self-esteem.
- Helping others is the surest way to learn about diversity and acceptance of differences.
- It is easier to concentrate after physical exercise.
- Differences complement.
- Physical fitness makes the body not only look good but also feel good; a healthy body is a real asset in life.
- Happiness is about self-contentment.
- Mrs. Hood was right when she said, "You always miss 100 percent of the shots you don't take."

24

Second Chances

"Like this, Daddy?"

"Yes, but if you hold the gun more like this," Dad said to his ten-year-old son as he showed him again exactly where to position the gun, "the backfire won't bruise your shoulder. Look down the barrel, line up your target in the cross hairs, breathe in and hold it, and when you feel confident about hitting the target bull's-eye, pull the trigger."

Pooooow!

"I hit it!" Tim shouted in glee as he ran to retrieve the rusty and now mutilated tin can. "Look, Dad, I shot a hole right through the center of it!" Tim felt now he was an excellent marksman. Like his father. Like his older brothers and sisters.

"Good shot, son," Dad said, praising his son's emerging skills.

"Please, Daddy, can I shoot at the ducks this time when you take me hunting with you this year?"

"Not this year; you're not ready, son. You'll need more practice. Shooting at a flying duck or at an animal running at full speed is different from knocking a tin can off a post. But after watching that last shot, I'd bet you'll be ready soon. Keep at it, and don't lose faith. You're never too good—or too old, for that matter—to practice."

Tim tried again. "Then how about taking me deer hunting with you next month? I'm a good shot and you said I'll get better, and a deer is a pretty big target! I won't miss."

"Son, big target or not, you must never, never shoot at a bird or animal that you feel you cannot kill in one clean shot. Anything less is cruel and wasteful. Hunting is fair *only* when it's humane and for a purpose. And there's more to hunting than the shooting part. You need to understand the habits and survival instincts of the animals you're hunting. Besides, Tim, we don't have a license for you, and you're too young to get one for deer, anyway."

The young, enthusiastic would-be hunter thought about his dad's words. "I have a great idea!" Tim countered. "You can take me deer hunting right here on our farm. You said yourself that the herd of deer that cross over our land by the creek bed are a nuisance because they eat and trample the outer ten rows of corn in the field. We can shoot one of those deer; that way I don't need a license, and you can teach me how to hunt deer so I'll be *really* ready when I am old enough to get a deer license! What a great idea, Dad. How about it?"

His son's enthusiasm made him smile. "Son," he said, putting his arm around my brother's shoulder, "I know you're anxious to hunt. I've been hunting one thing or another for nearly 25 years, and I still enjoy it. And I love to hunt with you. But I want you to listen carefully to what I have to say. You must never, *never* hunt out of season, even if the animal is on your property. That doesn't make it right. You must always respect the need for balance in nature."

"What do you mean, Dad?" my brother asked, looking confused.

"Well, there are some common-sense laws that you should obey. For example, you must never shoot females during the season of bearing and protecting their young; you must never hunt more birds or animals than you can use and that's allotted by the state's regulation for controlling the populations. Even though hunting out of season is illegal by man-made laws, you must learn to respect these laws, too. Do you understand why good hunters practice respect for these things?"

"Yes, Dad." The boy had heard these lessons time and time again from his father, and from his older siblings who by now knew them well.

"Tell you what, Tim," his father said, "we've got some muskrats sneaking up from the old creek bed, killing our ducks and chickens. How about you being responsible for those traps? Then, in fox season, you can take over the fox traps. The fox population is so large this year, they have just about overrun this county. They're eating everything in sight, including raiding our corn bins. They've been helping themselves to our ducks, chickens and geese all fall, and have just about wiped out the wild ducks that migrate to the water on the creek every year. I could really use some help trapping them."

"That's what you mean when you say it's okay to hunt when there's a *purpose*, isn't it?" Tim remarked.

"Exactly, son."

And so it was that my father taught Tim, as he had his other children, the rules of using firearms. And sportsmanship, a respect for wildlife, the need for balance in nature. And of man, animal, and Mother Earth co-existing in harmony.

My father, now 74, is keenly aware that he is entering his last quarter century of life. "Kind of makes you think you may not have time for second chances," he said to me recently, "just last chances."

I thought about his remark for quite some time because it seemed so uncharacteristic of my father. Dad was an optimist and a doer. Just a few days earlier my friend Roger Norman Jr., on his wedding day to Elise Alessio, said in a toast to his father, "Thanks for all the good times, Dad; we've had enough fun to last five lifetimes." When I heard him make this remark, I thought about my father and the way he lives his life, whether at work or play, making every minute count. My Dad is a man of action. He is purposeful and goal-oriented. I couldn't imagine any experience that he had missed; he lived life so fully. Surely he had done all he wanted to do, when he wanted to do it. I couldn't think of anything he hadn't done.

As I was driving into my younger brother's yard this past summer, I encountered a most unexpected sight. Several full-grown black bears were climbing the trees in his front yard, one bear was coming out of the rows of sweet corn in the garden, another stood on his back legs looking ready to pounce on an empty wheelbarrow nearby and a cub bear stood with outstretched paws raised in the air, looking very bewildered. Thirteen bears in all.

I pulled into the guest parking space and contemplated not getting out of the car. Within moments, my brother emerged from the house grinning from ear to ear. "I can explain!" he said. "You can get out of your car; they're only *plastic.*"

Plastic life-size bears in my brother's yard! I was sure he had lost his mind.

Noting my astonishment, my brother added, laughing, "You're probably thinking I'm nuts, right? I'm taking Dad hunting next month in Canada."

"Sounds exciting," I said. "How did that come about?"

"Last fall I noticed Dad looking over a hunting magazine I had in my study. He commented that hunting bear was the one thing he had never done, but had always wanted to do."

"Did Dad *really* want to go, or was he saying that it just sounded like fun?" I asked.

"That's what I wondered," said my brother, "so I asked. 'Oh, it must be a thrilling experience,' Dad said, but added something about 'I'll probably never get a chance, even though I would like to.'"

"If bear hunting is an unfulfilled desire for Dad," I said, "he should go. I mean, if he doesn't do it now, when?"

"Precisely what I thought," said Tim. "Dad may not get another chance. It's unlikely he's got too many bear hunting seasons left."

"Let me guess," I said. "*This* is the year for Dad's bear!"

"That's right, Sis," Tim said. "I applied for a hunting license for the two of us and when I learned we had each received them, I knew we had better practice. Dad's not been hunting for a while, and his eyesight isn't what it used to be. So I thought it best he have a chance to do some target practice to rejuvenate his marksmanship, timing and response skills. I saw these nice bears at a farm sale and bought them. As you can see, I've positioned them, strategically, for range practice. Pretty clever, huh!"

"It sure is," I agreed.

"I really want this experience to be a good one for Dad," Tim said in a concerned voice. "In all ways. Come, look what I've done to make it comfortable for him to practice from the trees. You may not know this, but with bear hunting, the hunter waits up in the tree, so I've placed a sitting pad—a padded cushion, no less—at various angles and heights in the trees here in the yard. Dad and I have been practicing every week, without fail. We're almost ready!"

In the Quetico National Forest, near Lake Eva, in the Province of Ontario, Canada, the 280-pound black bear looked my Dad square in the eyes. It became a match of survival of the quickest.

"What was the experience like, Dad?" I asked.

"Thrilling," he said, "*Nothing* short of it."

"I've listened to your father recount the hunting trip time and time again," said my mother. "What's clear is that not only was the actual hunting of the bear an exciting adventure, but the fact that the experience had almost eluded him—but then became a dream come true—was in and of itself an enormous added measure of satisfaction, zest and zeal."

This made me wonder how many unfulfilled desires my parents, either Mom or Dad, were harboring. I wondered how many experiences either had given up because of the life they had chosen, the path each had followed, what the circumstances of their lives together either allowed or disallowed. I thought about it in relation to my own life and the way I approach my life. I expect to do what I want to do. When a dream becomes a desire, I channel the desire into a goal and formulate plans to accomplish the goal. For me, following this philosophy leads to ample feelings of fulfillment. I want my chances now, not later. I know this was not the case with my parents. Throughout my childhood, I watched them make many sacrifices for the sake of us children.

I asked my mother if she had been harboring any second chances, or last chances.

"Oh," she replied, "I suppose there are some things that I wanted to do, but every year they get less and less important. Now other things, like time with my children and grandchildren and great-grandchildren, become more important. Well, maybe not more important, but as important."

"Oh, c'mon Mom," I said. "What was the most exciting 'second chance' you were able to live out?" I asked.

Nostalgically, she recounted a story of a time surrounding my daughter's birth.

My daughter was due to be born in March. I was a classroom educator at the time and wanted to resume my teaching assignment immediately after her birth, to complete the school season, which ended in late May. My husband and I lived in a lovely modern duplex. The building was in a pretty part of town and had a spacious yard with lots of trees and shrubbery. The owner, Mrs. Kyle, and her husband lived in the unit below, but had moved out in order to have their apartment completely redecorated. When completed, it was like a brand-new apartment. But Mrs. Kyle and her husband didn't get the chance to move in; Mr. Kyle became suddenly ill and died, and Mrs. Kyle moved to a nearby city to be closer to her grown children.

Since my mother had expressed a willingness to care for my newborn while I completed the school year, it seemed logical to rent Mrs. Kyle's apartment for her. My mother is a very private woman, and I felt that having her own apartment would give her privacy, so she would not feel that she was intruding in my family's home. It would also allow her to go about caring for my newborn at her own pace and in her own style.

My mother came to Des Moines to settle in the apartment, and on that very day my daughter was born.

The months that my mother cared for our daughter was a cherished time. I still have fond memories of my mother bathing her infant grandchild in the sink, talking and singing to her, taking baby Jennifer for a walk in the stroller in the neighborhood, going to and from the grocery store.

This was a very happy time for my mother. It was a very beautiful apartment, so I knew Mother found it to her liking. My father came and stayed for several weeks at a time, so neither of them ever felt disconnected from the other. It was more than apparent that Mother had fallen in love with her granddaughter, and that she enjoyed our frequent mother-daughter visits.

Mom was enjoying life—her *new* life. She stayed for three months, until the school year ended and I was able to be at home for the summer to care full-time for my daughter. Sadly, Mother said goodbye to us and returned to her home in the country.

Up until my father's "second chance" experience, I had accepted this version of my mother's happy experience. But now I was curious and wanted to probe deeper.

"Mom, what made it so *special* for you?" I asked.

"Oh," she said, her eyes lighting up, "I went from my mother's house to creating a home for my husband and children. I never really lived on my own, independently, until my granddaughter,

Jennifer, was born. It was my *first* time having an apartment of my very own, as I had wanted as a young woman. I can never thank you enough for renting the apartment for me. It was a chance to enjoy an experience that I missed early in my life. Now, I've done it."

This was an interesting revelation, because in growing up my mother was firm in her advice to us children: "Make time for yourself *before* your time belongs to others. Learn to take care of yourself and to know yourself *before* you take on the responsibility of caring for others. Create a place of your own *before* you make a home for others. And be careful whom you date; you may be choosing your mate." Mother was full of good advice and lovingly imparted it to her children, though she hadn't taken that route herself.

I wondered how many chances my parents had missed out on. They had lived their lives centered around their children and the responsibilities of family life, and I am quite sure that their needs often became secondary to the needs of their family. Choices and chances are often a product of time.

Time. Sometimes friend, sometimes foe; often time reminds us of its limited supply in each of our lives. In youth there's plenty of it; in mid-life there's a crisis for it; in the later years there's an accounting of it and a genuine appreciation for any more we are allowed.

When I listened to the *joy* expressed by my parents in realizing each of the second chances they talked about, I learned that they not only appreciated the gift of the experience because there was the possibility that a "chance" had passed them by, but more important, savored it precisely because the second chance/last chance was provided by their children—and this added a measure of sweetness.

Not just for my parents—but for us children as well.

As children, our lives are paved with opportunities provided for us by our parents. But it occurred to me that it is not just parents who provide opportunities; children, too, provide opportunities.

May we take inventory to see that the ledger is balanced. The sooner, the better.

25

Caretakers

"C'mon, Bettie," my Dad said, rousing me from my warm and comfortable feather bed. "I need you to go with me. We shouldn't be long."

Being picked from among the six kids to go with Dad on these late-night checks was a miserable drudgery, made easier only by Dad's nurturing demeanor.

I put on my coat in silence. I despised going out in the cold, and he was aware of it.

"Why don't you put my old overcoat over your jacket tonight," he said tenderly. "That should keep you warm enough."

I gladly obliged. I shoved my arms into the bulky coat; Dad tugged it around me and buttoned it up. He untied the wool scarf from around my neck, then lifted up the collar of the old coat and secured it with the scarf.

"Better wear some warm gloves," he said. "Here, take this pair of mine put them on over yours." Dad removed his gloves, handed them to me, and took out his favorite fleece-lined gloves from the hall closet. He put them on and then pulled on a pair of well-worn gloves over them. Noticing several holes in them, he commented, more or less to himself, "I can't wear these; the holes are so big my good gloves will get wet and dirty." He reached for a different pair of old gloves, examined them carefully, and finding them intact, pulled them on over his precious fleece-lined gloves.

"Ready?" he asked softly.

"Not really," I said in my best forlorn voice. I looked like a snowman in winter clothes but felt like a mummy.

"This won't take long," he said, trying to comfort me. "We'll probably be back here in 20 minutes or less."

We were about to go to the barnyards to check over the livestock to see how they were faring with the cold. Sub-zero weather made it dangerous for newborn animals out in the open.

Hearing our footsteps, and perhaps alerted to the smell of humans, the animals in the barnyard grew quiet as they strained in the dark to see who was approaching. Recognizing the sights and sounds as familiar, most animals resumed their general state of drowsiness, though some did not. Several clumsily got up and began to follow us, nudging my dad in the seat of the pants with their noses, and with their heads, they lifted up his arms in hopes of being petted. Others thought their bringer-of-the-food might have some, and so hustled to the feeding troughs.

Dad laughed at their antics and exchanged chatter with their bleats, bahs, moos and oinks, stopping briefly to pat the heads and rub the backs of some of his favorites, such as the goat who, the instant she saw Dad, bounced over and demanded a pinch of Dad's chewing tobacco. "No, I don't have any Skoal for you tonight, Millie," Dad cajoled, pushing her out of his way. The goat butted Dad a number of times on the side of his leg, hoping the playful tantrum would yield her a tobacco fix. "Go on, get," he told her as the goat continued to follow. I loved watching my father with his animals. Dad was a caretaker. And caring for his animals brought out the best in him.

As I followed along, Dad walked hastily through the barnyards, shining a flashlight into the crowds of animals huddled in for the night. When he scanned the flock of sheep, his watchful eyes discovered Annabelle, the old ewe. Tonight, out in the open barnyard, on the coldest night of the year, Annabelle was about to "lamb." She lay on her side, feet out, panting heavily. Instantly recognizing these signs as labor, Dad knew we had to get Annabelle to shelter. Though the ewe wore a heavy fleece of wool, her newborn would be born with only a wet coat of fuzz. Lambs rarely survived a night as cold as this.

"C'mon, Annabelle," Dad said, "Let's get you to the barn. You can't lamb out here. C'mon, get up. Let's go, old girl."

The old ewe struggled to her feet and took a few steps, but the burden of her enormous belly was much too cumbersome for her to walk further. Annabelle decided that she, not Dad, was in charge here. The old ewe lay down, let out a big sigh, and resumed her labor. There was little choice but to wait it out.

Momentarily rebuffed, Dad asked, "Annabelle, how come you've decided to have lambs at your age? I thought you'd have given up on that by now!" The old ewe looked at him as though she could understand him, but only momentarily. She involuntarily turned her attention to the work at hand.

"Okay, if you insist on having your lamb out here in this freezing cold," Dad said talking to her, "I guess we have no choice but to wait for you. Let's get this over with, and then we'll get you to the barn." Calmed by my father's presence, Annabelle leaned her head in the direction of my father's hand.

Within moments, the first lamb was born.

"That's quite a big lamb for an old girl like you," Dad commented as he rigorously dried the baby lamb with the old towel he'd brought with him—just in case he needed it for any animal who decided birth couldn't wait until morning. He rubbed the baby lamb briskly and handed it to me.

"Here, Bobbie (my nickname since I was supposed to be a boy), put this little guy inside of your coat, and we'll get this family to the barn. Keep the lamb's head out though, so Annabelle knows we didn't forget her kid, or she'll never go with us."

Determined to get all of us out of the cold night air, Dad commanded Annabelle to get up. "Okay, Annabelle, let's go. Let's get you to the barn." He encircled the old ewe with both his arms, trying to help her stand up. Wanting to please Dad, Annabelle lifted her head, but found it impossible to comply with his command. The ewe's breathing grew cumbersome, and she lay her head back down on the ground. Dad took notice of her actions. Instinctively, he knew what this meant. Dad looked alarmed. "She's going to have another lamb," he said.

One lamb was the norm, two lambs to any ewe was an event. That a ewe as old as Annabelle should carry any young was unusual; that she should have two lambs was a remarkable feat.

Dad observed the old ewe carefully; his skepticism was apparent. "It's not a good sign," he said, shaking his head. "For Annabelle, two lambs is bad news." Experience had shown him that for a ewe as old as Annabelle, either the lamb would be still-born or the old ewe might die in labor.

Kneeling beside Annabelle, we watched and waited. "You can do it, Annabelle," Dad whispered to encourage and comfort her. She didn't take notice.

Suddenly, her irregular breathing grew louder and her eyes showed her duress and pain. Out came the second lamb.

"Look at this," marveled my dad when he saw that the baby lamb was born alive. "Annabelle, old girl," my dad said, "he's not only alive, but big and healthy, too!" Once again, my Dad rubbed down the newborn, his eyes never leaving the face of the old ewe. Satisfied that the baby lamb was dry and that its circulation had been stimulated, he tucked the baby lamb inside his coat for shelter. Without wasting a moment, he reached down to help the old mother ewe get up.

"Okay, Annabelle," Dad said. "Now we're going to the barn. No excuses."

Once again the old ewe refused. Dad tried again. "C'mon. Up you go. I won't take no for an answer."

Annabelle said 'no' anyway. And pushed out a third lamb.

The old ewe had given birth to not one, not two, but three lambs.

"Three?" Dad asked, rather surprised that an old ewe had room for three lambs, and three live lambs at that!

But the third little lamb wasn't all that committed to living, and lay lifeless upon the frozen ground.

"Oh, no you don't," Dad said. "We left our warm beds and braved this cold, and we're not going to let you die on us. You get up and fight for your life!"

The baby lamb bleated faintly, just loud enough to let Dad know it wasn't as committed to living as Dad was to having it live. The little lamb sighed, and once again lay still. Dad pulled off the outside gloves, now wet and cold, and with his special fleece lined gloves—the ones he had so carefully been protecting—rubbed the baby triplet with them so rigorously that the little lamb cried, sending rich oxygen into its lungs. "How's that feel, little feller?" he asked the fragile newborn lamb. "Pretty good, huh. See, you'll make it. You'll find the world a pretty good place to be. I think you'll like it. You just hang in there."

This scene and conversation between this big man and minuscule newborn triplet was a touching one, one that left a lasting impression, even though I had seen my father rescue or help one animal or another many times. My father—the Mother Teresa of the barnyard animal kingdom.

"Open up your coat, Bob," Dad directed me. He pulled open the coat I wore and handed me the second lamb, tucking it inside my coat next to the first, pulling it snug around me. Dad then tucked the reluctant third baby lamb inside his own coat. Dad moved into high gear.

"C'mon Annabelle," Dad said softly. Without a trace of hesitation or rebellion, the new mother of triplets got up and willingly followed.

We guided Annabelle into the barn and put her and the lambs in a small pen, now covered with clean straw. Once there, Annabelle fussed over her newborn lambs, licking them and nudging them to suckle. Dad placed feed and water in the corner of the pen. He looked over the new family of four. "Good job, Annabelle," Dad said, commending her for her efforts. "That was truly remarkable!"

Turning to me, he said, "She'll take over from here. Let's get you out of this cold. C'mon, I'll race you to the house!"

"You're on!" I challenged.

As usual, he let me win.

Once out of our coats, we sat at the large wooden table in the kitchen, drinking a cup of hot cocoa.

"You really love your animals, Dad," I said. "You're so good with them."

"Nothing gets more satisfying than watching Mother Nature and being able to help out when needed," he replied. "I was at your mother's side when you were born, you know. Luckily, I wasn't *needed*, just wanted!"

"Are you still disappointed that I wasn't a boy?"

"Absolutely not. You're very special to me. Of all my children, you're the only one I was allowed to see being born. When your mom was giving birth to you they allowed me to be in the hospital room, but not for any of the other kids."

"Was watching my birth scary?" I asked.

"No, not scary. Birth is a such a spectacular and awesome miracle, that fear is replaced with a sense of reverence and awe. One thing is for sure. If you ever doubt that there's a God, birth helps you believe otherwise. I'm disappointed that I wasn't allowed to participate in the birth of the other kids."

"Well, welcoming new life into the world is becoming on you, Dad," I said.

I was 17 when Annabelle had her triplets.

"You're losing the rhythm, honey. Try to remember how we did it in class."

Class was the furthest thing from my mind; my body was progressing to the final stage of giving birth to our child.

Realizing that encouragement wasn't enough, he tried a

different approach. "Honey, that little babe we've been massaging and talking with for the last nine months wants to be born. I'm right here to help you. Just listen to my breathing. Follow along with me. Breathe to the rhythm of *my* breathing."

As though he could compel my labored breathing to comply with his natural rhythm, he leaned over me and ever so gently holding my face with his large masculine hands, put his head next to mine, exaggerating the sound of his breathing so I could hear his exhale . . . inhale . . . exhale . . . inhale. . . . This was natural childbirth and he sympathized with my duress and pain. He searched for a way to intercede. Maybe being closer would help. My husband, a 6'2", 200-pound machine—who earlier that day had tackled an opposing quarterback, sending him off the playing field on a stretcher—was practically inside the hospital bed with me. A tender partner, assisting his wife in their child's birth. Youngsy, as he is affectionately called by his family, friends and fans, was there—mind, body and soul.

Like all the other miracles of birth, *his* baby arrived. And when the magnificent little girl arrived in the world, her daddy was the first to lay his eyes on her, the first to touch her, the first to cry tears of joy for her coming to his family, the first to surrender unto her his unconditional love, the first to speak words to her post-womb, the first to convey a message of being welcomed, loved, wanted and protected.

When Dr. Minzter handed baby Jennifer to him, he gazed at her in awe. The joy he felt overwhelmed him, and his eyes immediately flooded with tears. He tried to talk to his new baby daughter, but there were few words that could adequately describe his feelings of what he had just witnessed, and none that could convey what he wanted to say to his daughter. So he did the next best thing. He showed her how much she was wanted, loved and needed.

As I watched, he instinctively did an unforgettable, spontaneous, heart-stopping thing. He lifted the stiff green doctor's gown he was wearing and hurriedly removed the soft, fluffy white button-down shirt he wore beneath. With it, he lovingly wrapped his new baby daughter in it, gently rubbing the smooth cloth against her soft porcelain skin, not so much to dry her or to keep her warm, but to soothe her.

And perhaps to shield her from the tears trickling down his face.

There is in that breathless moment after a baby is born an instinctual emotion that is too intoxicating to express in words and so gets played out in the eye contact between a husband and wife, spoken as she searches the eyes of the father of her newborn as if to say, "Here. Here is the miracle of life I've been hard at work on. Do you approve? Did I do alright? Do you love this precious little baby as much as I do? Can you feel the power of this moment as I do, and will you let it sustain you in our care—forever?" I looked to Dic, and though I said nothing, he understood perfectly my thoughts, etching within our relationship a mutual indebtedness that will be honored forever, regardless of the circumstances of our lives.

"Look at her. See our beautiful baby daughter. She is so perfect. Thank you for having our baby." He choked back tears of joy and love. "I love you and her so much. I will *always* protect her—and you."

It was a passionate and unforgettable moment. All his rugged and brute strength put to its finest test—tenderness.

Why did this spectacular dichotomy of strength and tenderness combined feel like déjá vu? Why did this loving caretaking seem so familiar? Where had I remembered the feelings of a man so tender, a man with such presence? With such a remarkable sense of responsibility for helping, assisting, protecting?

Dic carefully held up his newborn, nestling her safely against his big chest, holding her cautiously in place with one mighty arm. He placed the other arm tenderly around my shoulders, and along with Dr. Mintzer and the birthing team, walked his family to the aftercare room.

In that moment I remembered. My father had modeled the traits that became the criteria and standard I valued and respected in a man. Dic was like the man I watched patiently wait out the births of three baby lambs; the man who warmed them, talked to them and took them in from the cold—and watched over them as they grew and needed him in different ways.

Dependable, trustworthy, worthy. Dic. My father. Men you count on, in birth and in life.

"I love you, too," I said to my husband. "Welcoming new life into the world is becoming on you."

26 | Excellence Is Love in Action

On the wall next to the door of the principal's office hung a paddling stick with a bad reputation. This intimidating wooden board was displayed in the open for all students to see, a reminder that law and order was enforced in this building. You definitely did not want to get sent to the principal's office because therein court was held, and if you were found guilty of the crime for which you were accused, the paddle was used to carry out your sentence. I couldn't imagine being reprimanded in this way; Mrs. Hood, my teacher at Newark #7, rarely had to do so much as to raise her voice. We children never wanted her to be upset with us, so we simply did what she expected of us.

The stick had more than a bad reputation; Brian and Tommy and Henry and Clyde told us firsthand about the wooden stick. It was not just a *symbol* of justice. This paddle had seen active duty.

Mr. Pierson was the principal and the judge at this school. He was a very tall, very muscular and very handsome man with gleaming white straight teeth, dark brown eyes, shiny jet black disheveled hair and a shapely mouth. Unfortunately, good looks were wasted on this man. Mostly Mr. Pierson dressed in the same dark suit, alternating three bland and ready-to-send-to-the-cleaners ties to give the appearance he was wearing a different outfit each day (but we kept count and weren't fooled one bit). Every day he wore the same pair of never-shined, badly scuffed shoes. He always wore the same half-smile.

We understood that being a principal was very hard work and serious business, so when we children caught a glimpse of him—at those times when he did emerge from his office—we felt honored. And frightened. Mr. Pierson walked with heavy feet and with a long purposeful stride; when he passed by, you either felt in the way—sort of an uncomfortable feeling that the hall belonged to him and that you shouldn't be in it—or guilty, that the judge was coming to get you.

"How is your day going, Miss Miller," he said to my best friend Stephanie, one day as we walked down the hall on our way to the lunch room (I was pretty sure he had no idea what my name was). The two of us were so scared that we ducked into the girls' bathroom instead of going to lunch, afraid that perhaps Stephanie had done something wrong and was going to be hauled off to the principal's office for what the other kids described as a "come to Jesus meeting." I was terrified that Mr. Pierson might be waiting outside the bathroom door; and because Stephanie refused to come out I knew that if I came out, *I* would be sacrificed in her place. Lunch or no lunch, we stayed in the bathroom the entire lunch period.

Mr. Pierson's formal style was not limited to students; he wasn't very social with the teachers, either. Accordingly, teachers greeted him politely, offered up obligatory pleasantries, but didn't go out of their way to be in his presence.

This demeanor seemed to set the tone that was pervasive throughout the school. How different this felt from the wonder years of Newark #7, where cooperation with your peers was expected; here a spirit of competition existed—students competed with each other instead of working together and helping each other achieve competence (and have fun) in a particular endeavor.

Whereas at Newark #7 we needed every able body to make up a good team of baseball or whatever game was at hand, and were therefore all too happy to teach anyone a skill in order for that person to give a good effort, at this new school the mindset had more to do with exclusion than with acceptance. Gone was the goal of creating win-wins; now the task was about the art of sucking up to whomever was popular in order to garner status so that you would be asked to even play. Also gone were the days of co-ed sports; here boys played baseball only with the boys, and girls—who wouldn't think of playing ball with the boys—paired off in groups of two, excluding other girls who were not in their clique.

The old tasks of *doing*—helping the neighbor student complete her homework, fetching wood and water, raking leaves—were traded in for lectures on being good citizens. No longer were all your supplies stored in your one and only desk; now it was about remembering to retrieve just the right book from the locker several different times a day, for every desk belonged to everyone. Gone, it seemed, was the pride of possession. Only geeks kept their desks clean; the dirtiest, "gross" desk seemed to get the most attention and admiration.

The honor system of the cloakroom was traded in for a locker with a tough-to-remember combination, and the dearly loved Mrs. Hood was traded in for some seven-plus adults—some of whom taught subjects but not children, and some of whom liked children but weren't especially good educators. Whereas Mrs. Hood was judge and jury, in this school there was a master ruler, Mr. Pierson, who ruled our rulers—the teachers.

Unlike Mrs. Hood, who handled us with ease, the teachers here seemed to have difficulty winning the cooperation of the students and thought that getting us to learn was a matter of keeping us in line, rather than about the joy and fun of discovery. Whereas Mrs. Hood taught us how to learn and how to help each other work toward the common goal of mastery, now the task was to sit quietly without discussion or involvement with your peers. Worse, students were pitted against each other—such as having to raise your hand when you were done with your paper, causing fellow classmates to feel frustrated or dumb because they couldn't complete their work as fast as someone else could. This didn't seem to be very effective to me, and in fact, really unworkable. At this school, I had to work hard at being happy.

But I was hopeful that I could adjust, even if Mr. Pierson couldn't. He was going to night school to get his doctoral degree. The only doctors we had ever heard of were M.D.'s (not Ph.D.'s), so we students felt that it was because he didn't like us that he wanted to leave us—though we thought he would make a good doctor. At recess one day, third-grader Claude James got hit in the head by a flying baseball bat and was knocked unconscious. Mr. Pierson held Claude's nose and mouth and blew life back into his body. It felt good knowing that we were in the hands of someone who could keep us alive.

Because Mr. Pierson not only commanded respect but had a way of coercing it, we both respected and feared him.

When our regular music teacher began to show signs of being pregnant, she disappeared and a new music teacher by the name of Miss Thomas was assigned to the school. On her first day, she hung up a poster in our room with the words:

EXCELLENCE IS LOVE IN ACTION

Miss Thomas was the music instructor in the four schools in our county. Coming from one school to another, she arrived at our school every Wednesday after lunch—usually late. During these times, several classes joined together in the same room and she would teach us music. I thought Miss Thomas was wonderful.

Aside from being a good music teacher, Miss Thomas was a seduction of the senses. A delightful woman, she was always smiling, always joyful, laughter always resonating from her long, slender neck with the rather prominent Adam's apple. She was beautiful and feminine, and she smelled as good as she looked. Better than MaryLou Mericle, and much better than all the other teachers. Her very white and graceful teeth overlapped just enough to add a touch of appeal and intrigue to her smile. She wore her long dark hair in big loose curls and dressed in colorful stylish clothes that were, as Edith Head suggested, "tight enough to know that she was woman, and loose enough to know that she was a lady." With each ensemble she wore very high heels. On her long graceful arms dangled a bracelet, different with every outfit. All eyes would attentively watch as she slowly and carefully took it off and laid it gently on the podium next to her sheet music. Just looking at this woman was music.

Mr. Pierson thought so, too. It wasn't long before he took to visiting our classroom when she was in the room. If a note needed to be delivered to a student in our class during the time she was there, rather than having a student messenger deliver it—as was custom—he delivered it personally. We could tell he was making time with her. And it wasn't too long before she noticed. And approved.

By Christmastime she made a special effort to arrive to class on time, and soon thereafter, arrived at the school early enough to have lunch in the cafeteria—with Mr. Pierson. By Easter Mr. Pierson and Miss Thomas carried their lunch trays to his office, where they now ate with the door closed. Some of us children would hover near the office door, just close enough to see if we could overhear their conversations. We didn't hear anything but chatter and laughter.

The following fall on the first day of the new school year, the students were filled with enthusiasm for once again being with our friends at work and at play. And a very special first day it was. There standing outside the building, greeting all the students, was a very different Mr. Pierson.

We were astonished. There stood before us a man who looked more like a male model in the made-to-order catalogs than the Mr. Pierson we had known the previous school year. Besides being refreshing to look at, to our total amazement, he knew our first names and addressed each and every one of us. "Good morning, Bettie, nice to see you today," he said, looking directly at me. I hoped he hadn't noticed my obvious stare. "Good morning," I said meekly. "Good morning Jack, welcome back," he said to my friend and classmate, Jack Berryhill. Every student, called by name, was welcomed back to the new year. We students drooled with delight.

We took note of the fact that though Mr. Pierson was as tall as ever, he was even more handsome. The brown eyes twinkled, and the gleaming white straight teeth were now owned by a mouth with enough happiness to display a generous smile. His thick jet black hair was in the latest butch style, every hair immaculately in place. He wore a white starched shirt with a stiff collar, a bright and colorful (and clean) tie and stone cuff links. His fashionable dress slacks were the same as those on display in the store window at Spangler's Clothing For Men. New and newly shined black wing tip shoes with little black tassels complemented a black leather belt. Wow! One look at the new Mr. Pierson made the value of getting an education obvious. It was so you could be as cool, suave and debonair as he was. Or marry someone just like him.

Our chatter was filled with speculation about how long the transformation would last. It was hard to tell: the paddling stick that hung on the wall outside the principal's office had disappeared from sight. We wondered what had happened to it and concluded that it now hung *inside* the principal's office. We were too afraid to ask. In its place hung a poster with the words:

EXCELLENCE IS LOVE IN ACTION

We checked to see if it was the same poster that belonged to Miss Thomas or an identical one. The poster in Miss Thomas' room was gone! It had been replaced by a diamond engagement ring on her finger.

A new and improved principal, a missing paddle, a poster that had changed walls and an engaged Miss Thomas weren't all that was new. Mr. Pierson no longer *acted* as he had the year before, either. *This* Mr. Pierson laughed more, was more playful, and he now whistled all the time. He sat with us in the cafeteria at lunch time—as did Miss Thomas on the days she came to our school. He walked around and talked with students on the playground, occasionally stopping to push us high in the swings, or to take a turn at bat.

He no longer spent long periods of time in his office. Though he had never before substituted for a teacher when a teacher was absent from school, now he occasionally did. And he liked it. And he liked us students, too!

One day when he was substituting for Mrs. Fisher, he asked us to hand in our assigned homework and then engaged us in a lively discussion about his new favorite topic, *Excellence is love in action*.

First he asked who among us could remember the words on the poster. When finally enough students had ventured to repeat the poster verbatim, he asked, "What is excellence?" Too young to really understand what excellence was, let alone to recognize it in action, we sat quietly.

Mr. Pierson tried again, "What is love?" The girls giggled and the boys frowned. He looked over the sea of empty faces and realized that not one of us knew the answer. He tried again, "What is a friend?"

Now he was on to something. We felt like we knew the answer to this question, so when he asked us to name some of our friends we all raised our hands and nominated our classmates.

"Yes," Mr. Pierson said, "classmates are friends." But soon he realized that we were naming mostly those kids who in one way or another held power over the rest us because they could select—or reject—fellow students for things like being on a certain team on the playground or for a project in the classroom whereby one group competed with another (such as the spelling contest that was held every Friday), and so steered our search for friendships to those other than our peers.

"Who of the *adults* you know is a good friend?" he asked, followed by, "And how can you tell? How can we *recognize* friendship?"

Becky Faulkner raised her hand and said, "My mom and dad are good friends." That seemed like a dumb answer to us, so we all laughed, but it appeared to be the answer Mr. Pierson was looking for.

"Very good, Becky," he praised. "How do you know they are good friends? What happens between them that makes you believe they are good friends?"

"Well," Becky said in her Future-Teacher-of-America's voice, "when my brother has to go to Boys Scouts and I have to go to band practice all on the same day after school, my mother asks my father to take one of us while she takes the other and he says 'okay' without getting in an argument over it the way my friend Kathleen's parents do."

"Yes," replied Mr. Pierson, "that's a good example of friendship." To stimulate discussion he added, "Miss Bennet, didn't your mother take meals to Mrs. Hansen when she fell and broke her hip last year? And Miss Alexander, didn't I see your dad delivering eggs and milk to the Millhouses when their chicken coops were destroyed in the tornado last week?"

Deciding that he now knew the kind of the answers Mr. Pierson was looking for, Steve Smallenburger raised his hand and volunteered, "My dad is a good friend. When the father of the family living on the farm next to ours broke his leg last month, my dad and the neighbors helped him harvest his crops."

Seizing the opportunity to illustrate a point, Mr. Pierson said, "Mr. Smallenburger, your dad's sincere efforts at helping his neighbor at a time when his own crops needed to be harvested shows friendship *in operation*. And that's what excellence is: being the very best you can be, and helping someone else be their best." He then proceeded to give example after example of what our parents had done within the community that not only showed us what friendship and love meant in action, but also let us see that our parents knew and lived it on a daily basis. "Remember," he said in conclusion, "friendship, when practiced, produces excellence. And someday, children, you will *meet* someone other than your parents who by virtue of their loving actions, demonstrates excellence, and when you do, *you will know it*."

We already did. Miss Thomas looked like excellence in action. She had come and won our hearts. She had given us excellence, shown us love; and by loving us, brought forth our excellence.

Her loving actions had more than a spellbinding effect on her students. It had changed our principal and he had changed the school. Mr. Pierson's new sense of style and his new style of leadership had caused this school to come alive. The walls that were once stark were now virtually a mosaic of student works. Teachers buzzed with vitality.

Mr. Pierson had been right. It was easy to know when you were in the presence of excellence; and friendship, when practiced, produces excellence. What he hadn't known was that it would take Miss Thomas to bring it out in him. Their excellence, combined, had changed us all. We were drawn to them and wanted to be like them. And in good measure.

Miss Thomas and Mr. Pierson were married on the first day after the last day of school. We were all invited to their wedding. Every last one of us attended. In a long white dress our dark-haired Cinderella stood next to Mr. Pierson, surrounded by the entire school of children, all looking in adoration at these "excellent" adults.

If there was any piece of our hearts these two youthful, beautiful and loving professionals had not won over, it was clinched when Mr. Pierson hung their wedding photo, with schoolchildren included, up for all to see. There, where once hung the dreaded paddling stick, hung the poster with the words EXCELLENCE IS LOVE IN ACTION and next to it, the photo of excellence in action.

Not one single child in the picture was looking toward the camera.

Nor was Mr. Pierson.

Old Miss Mac

Miss Macklewein had a real knack for keeping the kids on their toes. She was a master educator and an ornery woman. This colorful eccentric taught English, and conjugations were her specialty. Miss Macklewein put the fear of God in all of us; we both feared her and liked her too, for that matter. And for good reason. Consequences were sure and quick. "Old Miss Mac," as the kids secretly called her, was an equal-opportunity teacher; she discriminated against everyone. While some teachers believed in the "don't smile until Christmas" theory of student management, Miss Macklewein simply believed in "don't ever smile." It really worked for her.

Miss Macklewein did not believe any student when it came to homework; hence she didn't feel the least bit of empathy for any excuse a student might give when any assignment was not completed and turned in on time. When Linda Rund said she didn't have time to do her homework because she had to watch her brothers and sisters while her father took her mother to the hospital to have the new baby, and when Steve Yoder told her he hadn't done his homework because he played in the evening's Junior Varsity football game against the Spencer Mohawks, in Spencer, Iowa, and didn't get home until 11:30, she said, "I didn't ask you *why* you didn't have your homework done, I asked *if* it had been completed. I'll see you after school!" Even when a student gave her a legitimate reason, like "I didn't do it because I didn't know how," it was no use. All excuses went unexcused. This sort of accountability meant we *always* did our grammar homework. It also stimulated a real buddy system. If *anyone* from English class asked you if they could copy your completed assignment for Miss Macklewein's class, you forked over your paper—because if a student didn't have his work done, the entire class was assigned additional homework.

This woman was a work of art—a perfect candidate to illustrate one of those humorous birthday cards where a cranky old woman on the cover doles out a sarcastic comment about getting older. She looked the part, too. Old Miss Mac's long hair was dyed pitch black. She wore it parted in the middle, with two braids— each going in opposite directions, wrapped around her head. We were sure that she powdered her face with white cornstarch. On each cheek sat two perfect circles of bright red rouge. Her tiny pursed lips were painted vivid red, as were her fingernails. This already imposing image was overshadowed by her trademark sheer black nylons with the heavy black seams running up the backs of her legs.

When she turned her back to the class to demonstrate on the blackboard the obvious simplicity of the elaborate complexity of diagramming, all eyes checked to see just where those seams might be heading off on this day! For some unknown reason the students took a great deal of interest in this. Should they be crooked, we would all look at each other and begin a round of uncontrollable laughter, all the while not letting Old Miss Macklewein think that she was the object of our witty humor. It was a mistake to be caught laughing; when her eyes fell upon you, you'd better stop immediately, because if Miss Macklewein saw you smirking, she would call you to the board and in front of everybody, make you diagram the exercises in the review section of the book.

Besides being a masterful educator, Miss Macklewein was very effective with her students. For her you got your homework done, you got to class on time and once in class, it was unlikely that you spent your time writing notes to your friends or doing anything else that would break your concentration from the work at hand.

It's surprising how much you can learn when you're paying attention in class!

My day of reckoning with Old Miss Mac came unexpectedly as I watched the school bus pull away after delivering 30-some other kids and me to school one crisp spring morning. It wasn't the sight of the bus that made my heart stop and my stomach seize; it was the realization that I had left my backpack carrying my precious, all-important English homework under my seat in the bus, and the bus was now on its way to the district office. I knew without that homework I was a *dead duck*, and because it was Friday *I* would be the scourge of the class, being the one responsible for a hefty homework assignment for everyone over the weekend. Not to mention the hours of conjugation hell I was sure Old Miss Mac would have in store for me after school.

A vision of Old Miss Mac's ornery old face and pursed lips filled my mind, and I knew I had no choice. Whatever it took, I had to get that homework assignment back, and fast! I looked at the plastic and steel watch on my wrist and calculated I had exactly nine-and-a-half minutes before the bell rang for English class. My plan of attack formed instantaneously. Run!

Without a second thought I sprinted through the schoolyard. If I could cut through the gymnasium, around the girls' locker room, across the basketball courts, down to the baseball diamonds and over to the football field, I could jump the back chain link fence, hopefully in time to head off the bus, flag down the driver, retrieve my backpack and run back to Old Miss Mac's class—before the bell rang!

My race with the bell was on, and I ran as fast as my legs and feet would take me. I became determination in motion. Unfortunately, my black patent leather Mary Janes weren't quite up to the task. I made it past the gym and girls' locker in record time, but when the terrain changed from the asphalt of the basketball court to the dew-covered grass of the baseball diamond, the smooth leather soles of my Mary Janes sent me tumbling down the hill leading to the dugout. The grass had just been cut and was left in large piles approximately three feet high and about as wide, ready to be collected later in the afternoon after it had dried out a bit. As luck would have it, my crash course placed me headfirst into one of those grass mounds. For a moment everything went GREEN! Now I understood why they waited until the grass dried to collect it. It's because wet grass clings to everything, and I was covered with it. I must have looked like the Loch Ness monster scrambling around on my hands and knees, sputtering as I tried to get the hundreds of blades of grass off me. And then I remembered—the homework, Old Miss Mac, the bus! I leaped to my feet, and once again the race was on. Panicked, I checked my watch; my green collision had cost valuable time. I had five minutes left. "I can still make it!" I said to myself.

As I ran over the 50-yard line of the football field I saw the bus round the corner, headed for my anticipated point of interception. Waving my arms, running with all my might and yelling to catch the bus driver's attention, I jumped onto the chain link fence and crawled my way up to the top of it. With my shoe wedged tightly in the chain link I balanced myself on the top of the fence, and swung one leg over to the other side. Now straddling the fence, I tried to swing my other leg over, but my Mary Jane was so tightly wedged into the chain link and my position so awkward, I was stuck. Again the vision of Old Miss Mac entered my mind, and a feeling of utter helplessness and doom ran through my body as I heard the rough engine sounds of the school bus pass behind me and continue down the street. Tears of frustration and dread streamed down my cheeks. I had failed, and to make matters worse I was stuck on top of the fence covered with wet grass and mud. All I could do was cry.

And then I heard a familiar voice. "Bettie Burres, is that you up there?" I strained to turn my body so I could see who was talking to me from behind.

It was Mr. Lewellen, the bus driver. "I just happened to glance up in my rear view mirror and saw you squirming up there. I figured you were after something pretty important. Here, let me help you with your shoe." He gently unbuckled my shoe so I could free my foot and helped me down off the fence. "Is this what you were after?" he said as he handed me my backpack. My arms flew around his waist as I hugged and thanked him. And once again Old Miss Mac's ominous figure entered my mind, and I realized I had ground to cover if I was to have any chance of beating the bell. So with a boost from Mr. Lewellen I was back over the fence, across the football field, through the baseball diamond, up to the basketball courts, around to the girls' locker room, left to the library and down the hallway to the second door on the right. I entered Old Miss Mac's classroom gasping for air, covered with blades of fresh green grass in my hair, and all the way down to my shoes. I looked as if I'd played nine innings.

As I slipped into my seat with seconds to spare, I felt an incredible feeling of accomplishment, relief and pride. It may have been a small victory, but it was a meaningful turning point for me. I experienced the jubilation of taking control of my situation and making something happen that seemed impossible—no excuses, against all odds, I got the job done, and had escaped the wrath of Old Miss Mac.

To my surprise when the bell rang, in walked—not Old Miss Mac but Mrs. Nelson, a substitute teacher. Mrs. Nelson explained that Miss Macklewein was attending a conference for the day. The class broke into laughter when Eddy Lane muttered under his breath that the conference was probably a witches' coven meeting.

I couldn't believe it. After everything I had just gone through to have myself and my homework to class on time, Miss Macklewein wasn't even there to enforce the rules. And yet, I was aware of feelings of pride and accomplishment welling up inside me. That Old Miss Mac wasn't there didn't matter; I learned the lesson I believe she, in her own style, intended to teach.

To this day, when faced with an insurmountable job, the vision of Old Miss Mac appears, and I can still hear her utter Rudyard Kipling's words, "We have 40 million reasons for failure, but not a single excuse."

I wasn't the only one who learned Old Miss Mac's lesson, nor am I the only one who admired her. Even Donald Kleppe respected her; and had learned more from her than any other teacher in his years of schooling, or so he said at the 20-year class reunion.

At first, I was surprised that Donald had been the one selected to do a tribute to Miss Macklewein, because on more than one occasion she had said to him, "I've shown you twice, how much more explanation do you need?" (What she really said was, "Just exactly how dumb can you be?") She expected an answer to the question. Not that Donald could give one. Grammar just wasn't his subject. She called Donald "The Mental Giant." When she needed to get his attention she would say, "Let's ask The Mental Giant." On cue all eyes turned in his direction, waiting for him to notice that a question had been fielded and that a reply—from him—was in order. Eventually he *would* notice that all had become quiet. With a look of sincerity he invariably asked, "Why is everyone looking at me?"

But on second thought, I realized that Donald *knew* her nature and so, by smiling sweetly and feigning innocence, he skillfully transformed Miss Macklewein's use of him as the butt of the joke into an out for not producing an answer to her question. Donald knew what he was doing.

"Old Miss Mac was a great teacher because she demanded excellence from all of us," Donald said in the speech honoring her. "Could that woman get our attention, or what! Old Miss Mac scared me to death. She had the congeniality of a pit bull." He laughed good-naturedly and then somberly added, "Old Miss Mac was great because she cared *so* much. We may not have thought so then," he said, "but she cared about her students enough to teach us about deadlines and responsibility. She was unwavering! I learned in her class first, and then again and again throughout my life, that we either make excuses or we can make the job get done, but we can't do both."

I looked at the sea of my classmates' faces at the reunion—all faces were smiling.

"To care about your students as much as she did is to love them," Donald continued. "If she were alive today I would tell her that it was she who was responsible for my success." After a long pause he said, "So, this is to the teacher who made us all wet our pants. To her 'shoot first and ask questions later' style. I loved her for it! I suspect the rest of you probably feel the same way. Thanks, Miss Macklewein." He paused again and added, "You were a real jewel. You made a difference in my life—then, and now. *I owe my success to you.*" And to seal his words, he held up his glass, a gesture of toast in her honor.

With that, the Master of Ceremony cleared his throat, wiped his eyes and stepped down. And the rest of us reached for a Kleenex.

About the Author

Bettie B. Youngs, Ph.D., Ed.D., is the author of 14 books translated in more than 26 languages. She is a former Teacher-of-the-Year, Professor at San Diego State University, and Executive Director of the Phoenix Foundation. Dr. Youngs is highly acclaimed for her work on the affects of stress on health, wellness and achievement for both adults and children; the role of self-esteem as it detracts from or empowers achievement, peak performance and vitality; and, stages of growth and development and their implications for youth, families and professionals.

To contact:
Bettie B. Youngs, Ph.D., Ed.D.
3060 Racetrack View Drive
Del Mar, CA 92014
(619) 481-6360

Give the Gift that Keeps on Giving:
CHICKEN SOUP FOR THE SOUL

Inspire the special people in your life with a copy of *Chicken Soup for the Soul* and *A 2nd Helping of Chicken Soup for the Soul*. Sometimes it's hard to find the perfect gift for a loved one, friend or coworker. Readers of all backgrounds have been inspired by these books; why not share the magic with others? Both books are available in paperback for $12.95 each and in hard cover for $24.00 each (plus shipping and handling). You're sure to enrich the lives of everyone around you with this affordable treasure. Stock up now for the holidays. Order your copies today!

Chicken Soup for the Soul (paperback)
Code 262X $12.95
Chicken Soup for the Soul (hard cover)
Code 2913 . . . . $24.00
A 2nd Helping of Chicken Soup for the Soul (paperback)
Code 3316 . . . . $12.95
A 2nd Helping Of Chicken Soup for the Soul (hard cover)
Code 3324 . . . . $24.00

Lift Your Spirits with *Chicken Soup for the Soul Audiotapes*

Here's your chance to enjoy some *Chicken Soup for the Soul* and the ears. Now you can listen to the most heartwarming, soul-inspiring stories you've ever heard in the comfort of your home or automobile, or anywhere else you have a tape player.

Two of America's most beloved inspirational speakers, Jack Canfield and Mark Victor Hansen use their consummate storytelling ability to bring to life their bestselling collection. You'll hear tales on loving yourself and others; on parenting, learning and acquiring wisdom; and on living your dream and overcoming obstacles.

Special Gift-Set Offer: All three volumes
(6 cassettes—7 hours of inspirations) for only $29.95 + S&H
(a 27% discount). *Best Value!*

Volume 1: On Love and Learning to Love Yourself
(2 60-minute cassettes) Code 3070 . . . . $12.95
Volume 2: On Parenting, Learning and Eclectic Wisdom
(2 60-minute cassettes) Code 3081 . . . . $12.95
Volume 3: On Living Your Dream and Overcoming Obstacles
(2 90 minute cassettes)
Code 309X $14.95

Call 1-800-441-5569 for Visa or MasterCard orders.
Prices do not include shipping and handling.
Your response code is HCI.

Gift Books to Warm Your Heart

Laffirmations
1,001 Ways to Add Humor to Your Life and Work
Joel Goodman

Joel Goodman, the founder and director of The HUMOR Project, brings you a totally new concept in inspirational books: *Laffirmations.* This little gem will inject humor into your life and work every single day of the year. Each entry starts with an hilarious quote from some of the funniest people alive or dead. It is followed by a question that will have you doubled over in thought. Finally, there is a tip on how to squirt the creamy filling of humor into the sandwich cookie of life and work. As a special added bonus just because we like you, there are twelve Ziggy® cartoons thrown in to keep you giggling. Put a smile on your face: read *Laffirmations!*

> Code 3464: paperback........................ $8.95

Mentors, Masters and Mrs. MacGregor
Stories of Teachers Making a Difference
Jane Bluestein, Ph.D.

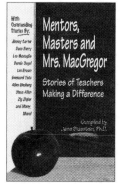

This book started with a simple question posed to thousands of people: Who is the one special teacher that made a difference in your life? Jane Bluestein, noted speaker on adult-child relationships, searched around the world for celebrities and common folks to answer this very question. *Mentors, Masters and Mrs. MacGregor* is a collection of their answers. Each story describes in beautiful detail for you the special connection that happens between a student and a real teacher. Some of the teachers are in classrooms, others are simply men and women who showed individuals how to become better people. This is a truly touching book that will appeal to the student—and the teacher—in all of us. The perfect gift for yourself or someone you love.

> Code 3375: paperback $11.95
> Code 3367: hard cover........................ $22.00

Call 1-800-441-5569 for Visa or MasterCard orders.
Prices do not include shipping and handling.
Your response code is HCI.